Raising Children to Achieve

Also by ERIC W. JOHNSON

Adventures for You (co-author)
Evaluating the Performance of Trustees and School Heads
The Family Book about Sexuality (co-author)
How to Achieve Competence in English: a Quick-Reference Handbook
How to Live through Junior High School
Improve Your Own Spelling
An Introduction to Jesus of Nazareth: a Book of Information and a Harmony of the Gospels
Language for Daily Use (co-author)
Learning to Achieve (co-author)
Life into Language
Love and Sex and Growing Up (co-author)
Our World into Words
Sex: Telling It Straight
Stories in Perspective
Teaching School: Points Picked Up
Trustee Handbook (co-author)
V.D.—And What You Should Do about It
You Are the Editor

Raising Children to Achieve

Eric W. Johnson

Illustrations by
Howard S. L. Coale

WALKER AND COMPANY/NEW YORK

Excerpt from A. Landers's column; by permission of Ann Landers and News America Syndicate.

"Helping Her Predict," *Learningames for the First Three Years*, Joseph Sparling and Isabelle Lewis. Walker and Company, New York, 1979. © 1979 by Joseph Sparling and Isabelle Lewis.

"My History in Clothes," "Moving and Saying," and "Seeing Feelings," *Learningames for Threes and Fours*, Joseph Sparling and Isabelle Lewis. Walker and Company, New York, 1984. © 1984 by Joseph Sparling and Isabelle Lewis.

"Why I Do Not Want My Child To Be Too Secure" by Anita Shreve. *Parade* magazine, August 14, 1983. © 1983 by Anita Shreve.

"Penny the Pup: A Dog Learns How to Hear for People Who Can't," by Susan Myers. Reprinted by special permission of *LEARNING: The Magazine for Creative Teaching*, © 1982 by Pitman Learning, Inc., 19 Davis Drive, Belmont, CA 94002.

"Rebecca Lee," "Charles Spaulding," "Roland Hayes," and "Jesse Owens," from the *Afro-American Historical Calendar*, editions of 1983, 1976, 1978, and 1981. Reprinted courtesy of George Beach, Inc.

"The Ghost of West Point," from *Reading Book 1* of the Kim Marshall Series, Cambridge, MA, Educators Publishing Service, Inc., 1981. © 1981 by Kim Marshall.

Susan B. Anthony story by Arnold Dolin from *Great American Heroines*, Lion Books, Publishers, Scarsdale, NY 10583. Published by permission.

"A Car Dealer's Unselfish Side," by Frank Rossi. Reprinted by permission of the *Philadelphia Inquirer*, August 31, 1983.

First published in the United States of America in 1984 by the Walker Publishing Company, Inc.

Published simultaneously in Canada by John Wiley & Sons Canada, Limited, Rexdale, Ontario.

Library of Congress Cataloging in Publication Data

Johnson, Eric W.
  Raising children to achieve.

  Includes index.
  1. Child rearing. 2. Achievement motivation in
Children. I. Title.
HQ769.J63   1984   649'.1   83-40410
ISBN 0-8027-0765-3

Printed in the United States of America

10 9 8 7 6 5 4 3 2 1

Contents

Introduction

PART I:

Achievement Motivation: Basic to a Good Life

PART III

Achievement Motivation and Some World Realities

Introduction

Perhaps the most common complaint of parents and teachers about their children and students is, "They aren't motivated." It is often said in other ways: "They don't seem to have any ambition"; "They just sit around and watch TV when there's so much to do"; "They don't have any goals in life"; "All they want to do is take it easy and enjoy themselves"; "They just follow their peers"; "Where's the good old American pioneer spirit?"

Why I Wrote This Book

I wrote this book to show parents (and teachers, too) how to raise motivated children—achievers. There's no simple formula, I assure you, for people are complex, various, and wonderful, thank God! But it can be done, and thousands of parents are doing it very well without any book at all. However, I think a book can help even parents of already-achieving children.

Achievement Motivation: The Basic Basic

I write with the conviction that "the basics"—to use that overworked word—are essential: reading, writing, figuring, speaking, listening; thinking clearly, being able to persuade and be persuaded; knowing literature, the arts, history, the methods of science and discovery, and the nature of the world, including geography; knowing how to behave according to necessary rules, at home, at school, on the job, in the community—both the rules of custom and the rules of law; and knowing how to work to get the rules changed.

But basic to all these basics is the desire, the motivation, to *do* and to do *well*, to set goals and work to achieve them, and to go on to further goals. Without this underlying *motive to achieve* none of the other basics is learned, except perhaps briefly out of obedience based on fear, or the desire to be good and stay out of trouble. So the single purpose of this book is to teach you how to help your children develop *for themselves* the basic motivation to achieve, to develop the attitudes of initiative and responsibility, always wanting to do a good job on tasks worth doing, and then a better job, and so to become a productive member of society and to enjoy the satisfactions that come from being productive.

How I Came to Write This Book

I grew up, and later as teacher, writer, and advisor to schools and boards, spent most of my professional life thinking that the desire to achieve was born in me, and in a lot of others, and I was thankful for that. Then about five years ago, I had a chance to talk at length with David McClelland, professor of psychology at Harvard, about his work on human motivation. (I'd known him for years but had never talked deeply with him about his work.) He taught me—and proved it—that achievement motivation is learned, not inborn. It can be developed very early, but it's never too late to start developing it, and it's not just the need for food and comfort—being "hungry"—that creates it in us. It's how we're treated, what's expected of us, how much and what kinds of independence we're given, and whether or not we're squelched by insistence on strict obedience as the first value, or whether we are stimulated by being encouraged: "O.K., try it"—with limits of responsibility to self and others. It's how we're treated, especially at home, but also at school and right on through life. As I said, it's never too late to release and stimulate people's motivation to achieve.

Having been so recently convinced of all this, and being an achiever, I thought, "O.K., so how can I use my experience as teacher and administrator and writer to get the word out, to help make people more productive, self-reliant, and satisfied by the usefulness of their lives?" I wrote up my ideas; McClelland and I got a grant from the Cleveland Foundation to pay me to spend a year at Harvard and traveling around consulting with experts and teachers of achievement motivation. I tried to learn all about it, and then I wrote three workbooks, *Learning to Achieve,* co-authored by McClelland and published by Scott, Foresman and Company, to provide schools with achievement-training lessons to be used at any level, from fourth grade through early college.

But people kept saying, "Yes, fine. But how about parents? Why not show parents how to raise children to achieve?" It seemed like a good, challenging goal, so I set out to achieve it. This book is the result.

How to Use This Book

First, mother and father, if both are in the house, read this book. As you read, if you have children old enough to talk, talk about the ideas you are reading. Don't make speeches, just talk, raise questions, and listen to reactions. If it sounds interesting to your kid or kids, let them read the book, too. Maybe they'll even help stimulate you to be more motivated to achieve.

At the end of each chapter is a section called "Putting It into Practice." These PIIP sections make up almost half the book and are full of specific suggestions for activities. You probably won't want to read them all until you've gotten a good grasp of the main ideas in the book. But glance at the PIIP sections just to see what's there. You might try some of them out as a way opens. They're all harmless; I hope most of them are stimulating.

As you read the book, observe your own parental behavior, and discuss it with someone (spouse, friend, relative, neighbor) in the light of the ideas in the book. Do you act as an achievement squelcher, or as a stimulater? If your children are old enough, maybe ten and up, perhaps even younger, discuss it with them.

Obviously, how you use the book will depend on how old your children are and what they're like. There are ways to treat babies and to interact with them, other ways with small children, and ways to share with adolescents. And if you have all of these in your house, even if you didn't beget them all, there are ways for them to react with each other.

The best way to use the "Putting It into Practice" activities is as opportunities arise or you create them. Probably a bad way is to command, "All right, sit down. We're going to do an achievement lesson," although that is certainly better than, "All right, sit down, keep quiet and listen. Here's what you've got to do, and I don't want any backtalk!"

I said "as opportunities arise." Once your mind is infused with the ideas in the book, you can use the approaches it suggests and the specific ideas in PIIP:

> at the dining table
> while doing chores together
> while sitting around before or after events
> while discussing the news, or your reading
> in the car, one-to-one or whole-family
> when friends, yours or the kids', come in
> when one child is observing another and you're watching
> on a walk or while jogging (between pants)
> at bedtime, anybody's

But sometimes, as with the organized games like Ring-Toss or Scrambled Letters, you will need to set up the game and play it in an organized way—or, better, let a child set it up and run it, with support from you as needed. The games in the book have mostly to do with realistic thinking about oneself, with goal-setting, and with various kinds of planning and keep-at-work ("striving") methods.

Also there are many opportunities for you and the family to put up lists, pictures, charts, clippings, message cards, and so forth around the house. If you have a bulletin board, a chalkboard, a bare-wall space that is Scotch-tape-proof, let them be available for use. "Putting It into Practice" will suggest how.

Acknowledgments
I acknowledge the help given to me, consciously or unconsciously, by the following:

my parents, long since dead, who bathed me with encouragement, let me be moderately naughty if it didn't seriously harm

anyone, expected the truth from me, set standards, and now and
then spanked me, but not very hard;

my wife's and my three children, who kept me in touch with
reality, including my own objectionableness, moved out on their
own, and are, at this writing, a pediatrician, an architect, and a
university administrative assistant specializing in publications
and graphic arts (with a free-lance graphics business on the side);

the thousands of school students I have taught over the years,
from slobs to the gungest of ho's, and their parents, who com-
pelled me to stay with the real world and were never (well, hardly
ever) dull;

the thousands of teachers I have had as colleagues, audiences, workshoppers, and wonderful advisers and arguers;

the friends and passing acquaintances at parties and gather-
ings who asked, "What are you working on now?" and when I
said, "achievement motivation," praised and condemned and
questioned the effort and made me clarify my thinking;

David McClelland, a major source of truth and stimulation,
who discovered much of what I show you how to apply in this
book. He has been generous with requested suggestions, and full
of faith. He has not read the manuscript;

Marian Chapman, one of the main creators and testers of the
Achievement Competence Training (ACT) program of Research
for Better Schools, who has been supergenerous when asked for
advice and has freely shared RBS materials;

Raymond Q. Armington, Cleveland industrialist, whose
pressing concern for the character education of American youth,
to teach them "initiative and responsibility" and thus strengthen
"the American way of life," has opened many doors and supported essential research and its publication;

the Cleveland Foundation, whose generous grant paid me to
learn at Harvard and elsewhere all about achievement motivation
and how to teach it;

Scott, Foresman and Company, who had the courage to
publish *Learning to Achieve,* and their editors Ann James, Lois

Teesdale, Jackie Miller, and Rosemary Peters, who benignly forced me to be clear, or just clarified me;

Dick Winslow of Walker and Company, and Walker editor Ruth Cavin;

my wife, Gay Gilpin Johnson, who sometimes says, "Come on, let's take a walk," and who, a vast achiever in her own work, agrees that married happiness is based more on complementarity than equality. (I'd hate to be married to *me!*)

—Eric W. Johnson
January, 1984

PART I

Achievement Motivation:

Basic to a Good Life

M*otivation,* as the word is used in this book, means the forces in us that make us act or behave in certain ways. *Achievement* means getting things done and done well. Thus, *achievement motivation* is the desire or urge to accomplish things, to do a good job at whatever we undertake, and, often, the desire to do a better and better job. Achievement motivation is basic to a good life, not only for any one person, but also for a family, a nation, even the world. It's the urge to achieve that keeps us productive and moving ahead. Achievement gives us self-respect. It is important, therefore, that we raise achieving children, at school as well as at home.

A pioneer in the field of achievement motivation is psychologist David McClelland, now a professor at Harvard. In 1961, his landmark book, *The Achieving Society,* was published. Its subject was how individuals and societies develop, or do not develop, high motivation to achieve. It dealt also with the consequences of achievement motivation. Since then, McClelland and his associates, and many others besides, have developed, tested out, and applied the information and theories in schools, families, businesses, and all sorts of organizations, among all classes, and in many nations. Scores of books and hundreds of articles have resulted.

Raising Children to Achieve takes the theory and practice of McClelland and others and shows how parents—in cooperation with their children—can put them to work to help raise achievers.

1.

Do You Really Want Achieving Children?

■ *In What Kinds of Families Do They Grow Best?*
Some people complain these days that too many children—and
adults, too—aren't well motivated. They seem to have no drive.
At home they spend too much time watching TV, eating, grumbling, and leaving messes. At school they hack around or keep
mum. In the neighborhood, they waste time or cause trouble, and
they stay out late. Behaving that way, how are they ever going to
amount to anything?

Other people complain that too many children—and adults,
too—are nice enough: they do their chores—usually; they do their
assigned work—if they have any; and they enjoy lots of friends.
But they don't seem to have any goals; they don't know what they
really want to do with their lives, except to take it easy and have
pleasure. They have no sense of purpose. How will they ever
amount to anything?

But all of us recognize that also there are children—and
adults, too—who are achievers. They have initiative. They are motivated to do a good job in whatever they undertake. They set

5

goals and work hard to attain them. They keep trying to find better ways to do things. They are self-starters and self-reliant. Yes, they sometimes relax; they know how to enjoy themselves. But one of their main joys is accomplishment. Also, they have a strong sense of self-respect. This self-respect is the basis for a genuine respect for others. It's true that they do not always do exactly what they're told to do, but that's because they have a sense of independence. They want to achieve their own goals, short-range and long-range.

The purpose of this book is to help you raise such achievers in your family.

■ *The "Natural" Drive of Very Small Children to Achieve*

If children are born healthy and well, they display achieving behavior almost at once. They wriggle and cry until they achieve the comfort of being held. Their mouths root around until they find something to suck, the nipple of a breast or bottle. A little later, they struggle to turn over, and sooner or later they win the struggle. They struggle to pull themselves up in the crib, and enjoy the accomplishment. They reach toward dangling playthings until they can touch and bang them. They have a goal to move from where they are to where they want to be—from alone to a parent's lap perhaps, or out of a parent's lap to something across the room. They manage to work their way to their goal. They wriggle along on their bellies, work their way up onto their hands and knees, and learn to crawl. What progress! But crawling isn't enough. They see people standing, even walking. They struggle to stand. They get some help, from a table leg, a sofa edge, a parent's hand—and they stand.

Standing is really something, but it's not enough. There's walking. And so the urge to achieve drives them forward: a step or two and a fall; a new struggle, standing again, more steps; and, at last, several steps from the edge of a chair across the floor to a parent's outstretched arms. "I made it! I walked!" What an achievement!

And so it goes: walking, running, climbing stairs. And of course there's toilet training—learning to control one's sphincter muscles, to ask to go to the special place, the bathroom. Studies show that children who are toilet trained fairly early tend later to be more highly motivated to achieve than those trained late. Of course, the training demands must not come too early, not before the children are physically able to control their urination and defecation. Before that, they should not be rushed into it. They may begin by telling you *after* they have had a bowel movement. Good! Praise them for that and you enable them to discover what they can do. You become an enabler as you follow the child's lead. But once they can and do control urination and defecation, they have learned to be a bit more independent, they are more aware of their own bodies, of the passage of time, of the location of the toilet. They feel in more control, responsible, pleased with themselves. And they get praise and smiles and encouragement for their actions, for what they have learned.

By age one, perhaps earlier, children can "say" by the expression on their faces, "I achieved it!" Certainly by age two and a half or three, children begin to be actively, verbally pleased with their own achievements. And one accomplishment leads to another, strength to strength, jobs well done to jobs well done, and to more-challenging jobs done even better. Learning to achieve seems quite natural, if the child is encouraged, given enough help but not too much, and is praised and recognized for each bit of progress made.

■ *How Families and Schools Can Squelch Achievement Motivation*

It is quite possible for families and schools to squelch the naturally developing achievement motivation in their children and students. However, *we know that it is never too late to reverse the squelching process.* We'll come to this in the last chapter, so don't be discouraged, no matter what you've done with your children up till now.

Perhaps the most effective and most tempting method for you

to squelch achievement is to put too much emphasis on simple obedience: "Do it *my* way, don't think for yourself." "*I'll* tell you what to do, you *do* it!" Many parents, at all social and economic levels, deeply feel and believe that they know what should be done and how, and that the key to success is for their children to do what they're told, promptly and right. Parents like these spend much more time in punishing their children with words or slaps for misbehaving or disobeying than in praising and encouraging their actions when they do well.

In slave societies, in which people are the victims of total injustice, where they are owned rather than owning themselves, the way to adapt successfully is to obey. Slaves know that if they get out of line, if they learn to think for themselves, if they set their own goals, they get slapped down, severely punished. The character drawn from Sally Hemings, the slave of Thomas Jefferson and others of his household, expresses the idea well in Barbara Chase-Riboud's novel about her: "I learned as a slave never to hope, never to anticipate, and never to resist, so I lived from day to day . . . trying to please [my] mistress [or master]—and keeping as quiet as possible."* If children are treated like slaves, only the most exceptional of them can learn to be achievers, to make their own way, to show initiative. All over the world there are still slave societies and millions of individuals and families in which the deep habits of slavery persist. These are habits of obedience, or of self-destructive, near-total rebellion; habits of blaming others, since you feel powerless to control your own life; or the habit of simply avoiding the issue by doing nothing. The challenge is for all societies to provide opportunities for all individuals and families to achieve on their own, to make it on their own, often against odds not of their own making, to become independent, responsible, productive achievers.

Richard deCharms, of Washington University, St. Louis, is one of the psychologists who have based their work on that of David McClelland. He writes: "Long discussions with . . . Mc-

*Barbara Chase-Riboud, *Sally Hemings* (Viking, 1979).

Clelland and his staff sparked my interest in motivation development." In 1976, in his excellent book *Enhancing Motivation* (New York: Irvington, 1976), deCharms uses the term "Pawn" for a person who acts like a slave, and the term "Origin" for one who acts like an achiever. He writes: "An Origin is a person who feels that he is in control of his fate; he feels that the cause for his behavior is within himself. A Pawn feels that he is pushed around, that someone else pulls the strings and he is the puppet. He feels the locus of causality for his behavior is external to himself. The motivational effects of these two personal states are extremely important. The Origin is positively motivated, optimistic, confident, accepting of challenge. The Pawn is negatively motivated, defensive, irresolute, avoidant of challenge. The Origin feels potent; the Pawn feels powerless."

■ Schools Also Frequently Squelch Achievement Motivation

Numbers of studies show that most children enter school feeling pretty good about themselves. But soon they learn that in school they must be quiet, follow instructions, do routine tasks whether or not they see any purpose in them, and do the tasks exactly the way the teacher instructs. If they think for themselves, they must do it secretly, or on the teacher's terms. Consequently, after a few years, too many children come to feel inadequate, or bored, or docilely obedient, or rebellious, or like dropping out—out of school and into life. But they have had little preparation to achieve in that life.

Fortunately, not all schools work this way. Many of them are able to build children up and teach them how to be self-motivating achievers, to be Origins. Chapter 10, "Working with the School to Strengthen Achievement Motivation," discusses the constructive, achievement-promoting teaching that thousands of teachers are doing, or can do, and how you can reinforce their efforts.

It is interesting that David McClelland and his colleagues have designed and carried out carefully controlled experiments to determine what sorts of teaching methods increase the achievement motivation of students. In Boston, Cleveland, and St. Louis, it was shown that providing specific training in achievement thinking and skills caused students to get better grades in later years, and to be more likely to graduate from high school than to drop out. And yet these methods have not swept through the schools. Too many schools have been stuck on subjects rather than working on motivating students to learn subjects.

Yet another way to squelch naturally developing achievement motivation of young people, or rather, to let it ripple out into nothingness, is for parents and schools to say to their children and students, in effect, "Be free. Just express yourselves." It must have been such an approach that led T. S. Eliot to say some years ago, "Too many of us think we are free when in reality we are merely unbuttoned."

■ *TV and Achievement Motivation*

One other major squelcher of and seducer from achievement motivation is TV, and the uncontrolled watching of TV. The main trouble with TV is not the content of its programs but the process of watching. TV is lively, jumpy, vivid, and absorbing. It tends to overwhelm thinking and imagination rather than to stimulate them, for the young viewer cannot, or does not, push a button, stop the tube, and say, "Wait a minute! Let me think about that." Readers or talkers can stop a book or magazine or conversation. They can think; they can ask questions, set goals, plan, assert their independence. But not so with TV watchers, especially when TV is used as a babysitter, a tranquilizer of family life, an escape from the challenges of exchanging ideas and developing social skills. It gives vast amounts of vivid information (and misinformation) but little chance to process it in the mind. Thus, parents who want to raise achieving children must control the amount of time the children watch TV as well as what they watch, or encourage the children to control it themselves. In addition, they should give their children lots of opportunities to talk and think about what they see. (Read Marie Winn's excellent book,

The Plug-In Drug: Television, Children, and the Family [New York: Viking Press, 1977].)

■ *Religion and Achievement*

It may seem quite a jump to go from TV to religion as we discuss achieving children, but the nature of a family's religious life may be relevant, and religion can be a squelcher of achievement or a stimulator. In *The Achieving Society,* David McClelland examined the effects of religion on achievement motivation over different periods of history. Certainly, it's a most complicated subject. As McClelland says in his book, "It is obviously necessary to go behind . . . labels to elements within each of the religions which may be more closely associated with achievement training."

McClelland then reports on the religious attitudes of the sects within many religions that have been conspicuously successful, especially in economic achievement. He found that in the Western world sects that "relied, at least to some extent, on tradition and on centralized church authority" curbed the impulse to achieve. Groups in which "the individualistic spirit persisted in purer form" were very often especially successful in business and in demonstrating the spirit of enterprise. Their ideas of mysticism, and direct contact with God, as well as reverence for life, caused them to work hard to make the world better—and more productive.

All of this is true not only in the west. In India, with religious traditions entirely outside the stream of Christianity, McClelland found the groups that were most spectacularly successful in business were small, minority sects, like the Jains and the Parsees. In all of these groups, in both east and west, an attitude of nonviolence and reverence for life was associated with business success. Also, a study of preliterate cultures showed that those that emphasized individualism, rather than strict obedience to religious experts imposing an authority and way of life from outside, tended to be more enterprising and interested in achieving.

McClelland explains: "The person with high motivation to achieve wants to be responsible for his own decisions, and the very

11

act of making a decision implies some uncertainty as to the outcome. He is therefore 'on his toes' ''—not safe, unrisking, and unthinking while performing all the correct prescribed rituals.

Of course, this does not mean that if you and your children belong to and seriously practice the teaching and preaching of this or that church you will necessarily be more or less of an achiever. But it does indicate that unquestioning, unthinking, strictly obedient, ritual-bound church-goers who are detached from the world and expect supernatural power to determine all that they do are less likely to be motivated to achieve. On the other hand, members of churches whose teachings lay on each member the responsibility actively to work to make a better world, to improve their own lot and that of others, are more likely to achieve. However, even within the most authoritarian churches individuals and families can find, if they *will,* much more room than is commonly thought for individual energy and enterprise. Parents can help their children, by example and discussion, to feel the urge, as a personal responsibility, to be active in good work and in working well.

William Penn, one of the founders of the Society of Friends (Quakers), is quoted in a Catholic leaflet called *The Quakers,* thus: ''True godliness does not turn men [and women] out of the world but enables them to live better in it, and excites their endeavors to mend it.'' McClelland also stresses the fact that minority sects, or those that rebel against tradition, are thereby setting higher standards of performance for their children. Concern for *religious* improvement (perfection) spills over into other walks of life. The excited endeavor to mend the world could almost be a synonym for achievement motivation. This would be a good subject to talk about with your children.

■ *The Characteristics of Families Who Raise Achievers*
Families that tend to raise achievers do not follow a single, easily described model. If they did, what a dull life it would be! Achiever-raising families appear among all races and classes and religious groups, and they exhibit all sorts of personalities. And so

do the achievers they raise. But there are characteristics these families tend to have in common. The mother and the father tend to *set high but appropriate standards of achievement* for the children and to *expect their children to achieve them*. They set the standards at as early an age as the children are likely to be able to meet them, with encouragement and possibly some help. But they don't set the tasks and standards so early that the children have no chance to do the tasks according to the standards.

For example, to expect children to make their own beds at age three would in most cases be expecting the impossible. Three-year-olds can't make a bed very well, and all they'll learn from insistence that they do so is that they're not much good and should be discouraged about themselves. But to expect three-year-olds to put away their toys so they won't be in people's way, or to throw scraps in the wastebasket, or to build a simple tower of blocks, or draw a colorful scribble on a piece of paper, or to put a toy car through a doorway without scraping the paint off, or to say some clear sentences—these might be reasonable challenges. Thus, achiever-raising families tend to expect their children to achieve things that will be a challenge to them, but not an impossibly difficult challenge.

So what about helping children as they strive to achieve a goal? Achiever-raising parents are *ready to help, but not too soon*. Children need to learn to try hard, to try different ways, say, to inflate a balloon and tie the end so that the air won't escape. A parent may say, "Here's a way to do it," demonstrating, "Want to try it that way?" That develops the ability to achieve. Or the parent might just say, "What about that rubber band? Could you use that?" These would probably be helps that strengthen the child's achievement motivation, especially if each one is followed by, "Now, you try it," or even, "Maybe you can think of an even better way."

Help that weakens would be for you to say, "Here, I'll do it for you." Then you do it. "There, isn't that nice!" That teaches the child to find somebody to do it for her or him.

And so the right approach—setting, or getting the child to

set, challenging but not impossible goals; giving needed but not weakening help—can be used all the way through the child's growth, from crawling, to walking, to block-building, to getting dressed and undressed, to cooking, to model-making, to tool-using, to caring for one's possessions, to riding a bike, to earning money to buy something the child wants or needs. The more you can free your children and encourage them to set their goals and to plan and work in their own ways to achieve them, the better. I'll say more about all this in later chapters.

There is a third major element in developing the desire and capacity to achieve: *giving positive feedback.* Achiever-raising parents get great pleasure from their children's achievements and successes, and from a child's efforts to succeed, and they make their pleasure clear. There's lots of hugging and back-patting when goals are achieved, with a big smile and a "That's great!" or "Wow!" or "Good job!" In quieter, less demonstrative families, there are subtler ways of saying "Good job!" by expression or gesture or words. It's important to notice that the emphasis is not, "You're a fine girl for doing that!" Children should never be evaluated as people; the emphasis should be on what they have done. "That was a great job you did!" This kind of realistic, honest, enthusiastic enjoyment of and praise for challenging jobs well done should go right on through life, insofar as we can provide it.

Sometimes, of course, children, like all of us, fail to achieve a goal they have set even though they worked hard and well for it. These situations I call *unavoidable failures.* For example, a girl tries out for a part in a school play. She reads her lines well, looks right for the part, attends rehearsals regularly. But there's another girl who's at least as good, and she is chosen. Here again positive feedback is important. "Of course you feel discouraged. Who wouldn't?" "Well, you worked hard and intelligently and made a good try." "This isn't the only play. There'll be others." "Did you learn anything from the experience that might help you do even better next time?" Give encouragement for what the child learned. (See Chapter 8, "Achievers Evaluate Their Performance," for more discussion of unavoidable failures.)

* * *

When I shared with David McClelland my preliminary plan for this book, he generally approved of it. But he pointed out a problem with many "how to" books: " 'How-to' manuals can produce horrendous, interfering parents. The books *could* be just new gimmicks for controlling kids." He went on: "Be sure to emphasize that parents have to *let go;* they have to let the kid set his or her own goals, make mistakes—but parents should be *sure* that the kid gets feedback. PATIENCE, PATIENCE! There is an achiever in every kid, no matter how hidden."

McClelland continued: "And be sure parents see the importance of supporting their kids in the goals they set, *because* the kids themselves set them, even if the parents don't especially approve of them (and provided, of course, the goals are not positively harmful). Here's an example: Years ago, our twin sons Dunc and Nick saved their pennies to buy a tiny TV set on their own because we refused to have TV in the house. We did not make them take the TV back when they reached their goal and bought it. We were really *pleased* at their initiative, so pleased that we pitched in a few more dollars to help them buy a better set, even though we still didn't approve of TV and regulated the amount they watched it." (Note: Both Dunc and Nick are now effective, high-achieving men.)

Perhaps you will be made a little fearful by what McClelland writes. "Does he mean," you may ask, "that I've got to let my children do whatever they want to? Do I have no influence over the goals they set? What about the simple good behavior and routine rules and tasks that make it possible for a family to live happily together, or at least not drive each other mad?"

Don't worry. Achievers are not generally raised out of chaos (although chaos has produced a few). In Chapter 9, "How Achievers Deal with Goals and Rules Imposed by Others," I discuss how people can accommodate themselves to the necessary demands of home and school and job, and still develop their achievement motivation and skills.

* * *

15

Achievement Motivation: Basic to a Good Life

Perhaps here it will be sufficient to quote a letter to the syndicated columnist, Ann Landers, and her reply:

> Dear Ann Landers:
> I am 15 years old and my biggest problem is my mother. All she does is nag, nag, nag. From morning till night, it is: Turn off the TV. Do your homework. Wash your neck. Stand up straight. Go clean up your room. How can I get her off my case?
>
> —Pick, Pick, Pick
>
> Dear Picky: Turn off the TV. Do your homework. Wash your neck. Stand up straight. Go clean up your room.

Let's summarize. One sort of parents who are likely to raise non-achieving children are those who dominate them, whose domination is ever-present, who emphasize strict obedience, and for whom a rigid "Do it *my* way" is the primary goal they impose on their children. These parents are authoritarian and tend to depend on punishment for the child who gets out of line. "Niceness" and conformity are praised; independence and achievement are not. Or, at the opposite extreme, such high standards of achievement are set that the children are almost bound to fail and, when they fail they are punished or rejected or disdained.

A less prevalent kind of raiser of non-achievers are the "just express yourself and be free" parents. Their children's lives have little structure, little feedback, little realism, and a kind of generalized praise no matter what the kids' behavior may be.

Achiever-raising parents, on the other hand, set reasonably high standards for their children, aware of what each child is capable of at his or her age. They let their children set many of their own goals and give them plenty of realistic feedback and support as the children work to achieve the goals. They try to make help available when it's really needed, but they do not over-interfere in the achievement process. And, very important, the parents feel and *express* genuine emotional pleasure in their children's attainments and the progress their children make toward reaching their goals. They give honest positive feedback.

There is one more point to emphasize here. Achievement motivation and skills can be considered "the basic basic," yes, but they are not all of life. There is humor and enjoyment in families that achieve; there should be time for relaxation, love, laughter, and play. It's true, let's face it, that some achievers seem dull and grimly determined. They need not be. Studies of the lives of high achievers show that these people tend to lead satisfying lives. Compared to those who are not achievement motivated, more of them are successful in the occupations they choose, or even in those jobs into which circumstances push them. They tend to show upward occupational mobility. They enjoy working and accomplishment, and their enjoyment is contagious. They enjoy leisure, too, but one of their main pleasures is productive, high-quality effort and accomplishment. It's interesting to know that achievers, all other things being equal, are less likely to be involved in traffic accidents and violations, are more likely to attend church regularly than are non-achievers (not that church attendance itself promotes achievement), are less likely to be drug users or alcoholics. They enjoy better mental health, and more of them report enjoying a sense of well-being than do non-achievers.

■ *Putting It into Practice*

Note: At the end of each chapter, you will find a number of exercises, activities, questions, and games that you can do with your children, or that children can do by themselves, called "Putting It into Practice." Obviously, how you use this material will depend on the age of the children and their ability to speak, read, and write. If your child is three or under, you will mainly be observing, interacting with, encouraging, and enjoying your child, and perhaps jotting down what happens. If the child is from three to five years old, some of the activities can be done on a parent-read, child-talk basis. From age six and up, children and adolescents will be able to do many of the activities more independently. In general, the more naturally you can work the "Putting It into Practice" exercises into the ongoing life of the family, the better, so that they are a part of the fabric of life rather than lessons. However, willingly done lessons are far better than nothing, and, if children help pick their own lessons out of interest, they often work very well.

It may even be that no children at all are involved, but that you hope that you, yourself, may become a more achieving person. In that case, you and other adults may use the book and these exercises to provide yourselves with achievement training.

1. What examples of achievement motivation can you find for any member of your family? Think especially of goals that your children have set, consciously or unconsciously, worked for, and achieved. Make a list and discuss it with anyone interested.

2. If you have a child aged three or under, think back over your memories of the child's life and note down goals the child has achieved. If you have an older child, find a time to talk together about the child's achievements during the first three years of life. Together, make three lists:

goals achieved

facts of family life that encourage achievement

facts of family life that discourage achievement

3. Look through family photographs and share with your children any that show faces that express achievement. What was happening in each picture?

4. Discuss with members of your family, or people who know your family well, the questions, "Does TV strengthen or weaken people's urge to achieve worthwhile goals on their own?" Have people list as many points on the *yes* and the *no* sides as possible. Then raise the questions: "Would our home be a more achieving one if we had no TV?" and, perhaps, "Should we keep our TV?"

5. Jot down a list of the specific examples of positive feedback members of the family can think of in the past week. Try to be specific: "Dad looked really pleased when he saw that Rita had fixed the loose back step so well and he said, 'You're a good carpenter!' " Are there any examples of children providing feedback to each other? Are there examples of child providing feedback to adults for definite goals achieved? Remember, in feedback

what you're thinking about is not the "Gee, you're great!" kind but, rather, "That's a fine job!" or "I really like that!"

6. This is for a baby, between about eight months and fourteen months old. It's taken from an excellent book, *Learningames: for the First Three Years: A Guide to Parent-Child Play,* by Joseph Sparling and Isabelle Lewis (New York: Walker and Company, 1979).

Letting Him Choose

Interesting things can happen when you give the baby a chance to make choices. Instead of just putting his spoon beside his cereal bowl, hold it up with another thing like a popsicle stick. Let him choose what he needs. Whichever he chooses, he gets to try to eat with it [choosing the means to achieve a goal]. Laugh with him about the silly things that happen when he chooses the stick. Encourage him to choose again. Give him other choices to make. [This gives] the child a chance to select the tool that is most useful for the task.

7. *A Case for Discussion*

Together or separately, read this story, which was reported in *Time* magazine of July 4, 1983, and then discuss the ways positive feedback is used to encourage achievement.

In 1981, Diamond International, a small company in Palmer, Massachusetts, that makes paper egg cartons, was having difficulties making a profit. Relations between management and labor were poor. According to a survey, 65% of the 325 employees felt management treated them disrespectfully; 56% were pessimistic about their work; 79% felt they were not rewarded for doing a good job. There were many worker grievances, much low-quality work, and productivity was low.

So management introduced something called the 100 Club. Employees are given points in recognition of above-average performance. You get 20 points for a year without an industrial accident, 25 points for a year's perfect attendance. Each year a record of each employee's points is sent home. When a worker reaches 100 points, he or she gets a nylon jacket with the company's logo and "100 Club" on it. Scores above 100 are rewarded with gifts such as blenders, wall clocks, cribbage boards—not expensive gifts, but meaningful recognition. Daniel Boyle, DI's personnel director, said in 1983, "For too long, the people who have got the majority of attention have been those who cause problems." Now, he says, good employees get the attention.

The result after two years of the program was that grievances were down 72%, time lost to industrial accidents down 44%, quality-related errors down 40%. Productivity was up 16.5% and profits were way up.

How was positive feedback used at Diamond International and with what results? Are there any lessons in this story for family life?

8. Write a story, or tell about a real happening, about an Origin and another about a Pawn. (See page 9.)

9. Give five examples of positive feedback that you've had from some member of your family in the past week.

10. Give five examples of positive feedback that you've *given* to members of your family in the past week. If you haven't given that many, discuss with the others whether there have been situations where you missed a chance to do so.

2.

What Is Achievement Motivation?

■ *It's Learned, Not Inborn*

There are some drives and motives that are instinctive. They are born in us, and we don't have to learn them. When we are hungry, we are motivated to find food and eat it; when we are thirsty, we are motivated to find something that will quench our thirst. When we are threatened by something, we are motivated to flee from it, defeat it, or come to terms with it. When we feel we need anything, we are motivated to get it, ask for it, or make it. We are motivated by the need to be sheltered from cold or heat or wind or other dangers. We want to be secure. We are also motivated to want good feelings: babies want to be cuddled and loved; children, adolescents, adults, and old people do too. And we are motivated to find sexual satisfaction. Of course, how, when, and where we satisfy these drives and motives involves a lot of learning, not just simple physical drive.

■ *Motives That Are Learned: Social Motives*

Human motivation is a complex subject because human beings are intricate creatures, living in a natural world that they have modified in complicated ways. Human beings also live in societies, and these are vastly complex. Therefore, it is not a simple matter to organize the motivations that we learn, our *social motives,* into categories or classes. However, it is useful to try to do so. One of the best methods of categorizing them has been developed by David McClelland and other psychologists and social scientists who have worked with him or have used his ideas and developed and tested them. This development and testing has been done with many groups of people, at many social levels, with all races, and all over the world in different cultures and different countries. The literature and records of human behavior over the history of humankind have also been studied and analyzed and tested retrospectively. Read McClelland's *The Achieving Society* for a fascinating account of all this.

According to McClelland, it helps in understanding human motivation to divide our learned motivations into three categories: the *achievement motive,* the *affiliation motive,* and the *power motive.* All of us are affected to a greater or lesser degree by all three of them. These motives are labeled "need for achievement," "need for affiliation," and "need for power" (in the jargon of psychologists, *n* Ach, *n* Aff, and *n* Pow. In this book, I won't use these terms, but simply plain English, but it may be helpful for you, the reader, to be aware of them).

■ *The Three Social Motives Defined*

Achievement motivation, as I have already explained, is the desire to achieve, to do a good job at whatever we undertake. The desire to perform well and then to perform better is the prime test of it. In a moment, I'll describe in quite practical detail the characteristics of high achievers.

Affiliation motivation is the desire to establish close friendly relations with other people, to get along well with them, to be liked by them. People who have high affiliation motivation are concerned about separation from friends or the disruption of relationships. They see group activities not primarily as productive, but as social. They tend to have many friends, to keep in touch with them, to avoid being alone. They put people before tasks, they need to be liked, they nurture and support others, and they tend to communicate with others about their feelings and others' feelings.

Power motivation is the desire to feel strong, to have influence over and impact on others, and to be seen by others as having power and influence. People with high power motivation think about how to exert power, how to gain status and reputation. They seek positions of leadership and enjoy organizing and managing others. Sometimes they go into politics. They tend to be outspoken, to try to influence others, to use information and resources to control others. In our society, they are very much interested in money, social position, and in collecting and using objects that will give them prestige.

I'm not saying that a person "ought" to be highly motivated to achieve and not have high affiliation or power motivation. In everyone, all three motives are present, and one or another may be stronger in some situations than in others—for instance, at home, in school, on the job, in the community—and at some periods in people's lives than at others. People's motivations and levels of motivation are constantly shifting. The purpose of this book is to deal with what I have already described as basic to a satisfactory, productive life: the motivation to achieve and the skills that enhance it. We shall be concentrating on that and how to develop and encourage it in children and adults.

■ *Some Characteristics of High Achievers*

As I have said, achievers come in all races, nations, religions, cultures, climates, and economic groups. They include men and women, people with low IQ scores and high IQ scores, young people, middle-aged people, and old people. However, the careful studies made of achievers enable us to say that they tend to share a good many of the following characteristics. As you read the list, it will be useful to try to stand off and observe your own family and see if you think its climate, activities, and interactions tend to foster these characteristics and to what extent different members of the family show them.

Achievers are self-reliant and reasonably self-confident. They take initiative and don't wait to be told what to do. They are self-starters. They are, to use deCharms's terms, Origins, not Pawns. They feel self-confident, but *realistically* so. For example, a ten-year-old, high-achieving girl would probably not be confident that all by herself she could organize and put on a dinner party for her parents and ten of their friends; but she might well be confident that she could make the dessert for that dinner and wait on table; or that she could learn to fix sticking doors, or put new washers in the faucets of the house she lives in.

Achievers are realistic about their strengths and weaknesses. They are not wishful thinkers. They look realistically at themselves and think realistically about their past performance. They remember the goals they achieved and the goals they were unable to achieve. For example, a fifteen-year-old boy who had never finished in the first half of a group of cross-country runners would not claim to be a top runner. On the other hand, if he had been able to assemble new bicycles and to repair household equipment for his family, he might well set as his goal getting a job as helper in an auto repair shop during the summer or on weekends.

Achievers feel responsible for their own actions. If they achieve a goal, get something done and done well after a good effort, they feel a sense of satisfaction in their own good work. If they fail to achieve a goal, they don't make excuses or blame bad luck or other people. They feel responsible and take the responsibility.

Achievers set challenging but possible goals. They set *medium-risk* goals, not easy, not impossible. They like the challenge of working hard toward goals that demand their best effort. They are good at calculating the possibilities of success. For example, if a brother and sister had succeeded last weekend in selling $25 worth of lemonade at a profit of $7, they might set a goal, with improved methods, of sales of $35 next weekend and a profit of $10. They would not be satisfied with just the same $25 and $7, or less. There would be no challenge in that.

Achievers plan carefully and intelligently. They look forward and figure out what tasks they will have to accomplish to reach a goal. They set the tasks in order, think about the resources they will need, work out some sort of schedule, plan for contingencies.

Achievers take obstacles into account as they plan and work toward their goals. Often, to achieve a challenging goal requires overcoming obstacles or finding ways around them. There are obstacles inside the achiever *(personal obstacles)* like social timidity, small size, fear of heights, inability to resist watching TV; and there are obstacles outside the achiever *(world obstacles)* like rules against doing what you've set out to do, opposition of others, shortages of needed supplies or funds. Achievers face and strive to deal with such obstacles.

Achievers know how to find and use help. Being realists, they know they can't always do everything entirely on their own. They find and use the kinds of help that strengthen them and move them toward achieving their goals. For example, if a couple of eight-year-olds wanted to use a heavy old discarded wooden ladder in the back yard in order to reach the branch of a tree on which they plan to build a tree house, they would probably examine the ladder first to find out if they judged it to be long and strong enough. But then they would get permission and ask their parents, or someone bigger than they, to help them get it propped up on the branch and held tight while they tied it on. But achievers would not just ask their parents to buy them a new ladder or to make the tree house for them.

Achievers are good at keeping working toward their goals—good at striving. They don't waste time, because time is valuable to them. They use time efficiently. They devise various methods to help themselves keep working. For instance, they often divide their work into accomplishable tasks, or they may promise themselves a reward after they have kept at work for a certain period of time.

Achievers check their progress. They are not wishful thinkers. They like to have clear evidence that they are achieving their goals. They see to it that they get factual feedback from others or from their own checking system. For example, if a young boy's goal were to run a mile in seven minutes, he would use a stopwatch and note down his times each day to see how well he was progressing.

Achievers enjoy achieving and dislike not achieving; they keep themselves at work by imagining how good it will feel to succeed and how much they will dislike not succeeding. They imagine feelings of success and failure. Thoughts about achieving, about goals reached and the satisfactions that come from these goals, loom large in the minds of achievers. When they write stories or interpret pictures, for example, they use many achievement events and words and phrases.

Achievers want to do a better and better job, or to do jobs in better and better ways. They like inventing new, improved ways to reach their goals. For example, if a child's job is to keep a good-sized pile of firewood beside the stove or fireplace, she may figure out whether it is more efficient to carry the wood, armload by armload, from the yard to the door, open the door, and then go through it to the fireplace, or whether doing the job in stages of piling and door-propping will work better. She will also try to figure out the best, quickest way to get the most wood into the available space.

Achievers use the goals they achieve as a basis for new goals to set and achieve. One goal leads to another. Achievement motivation is like a muscle; the more you use it, the stronger it grows.

■ *Achievers and Money*

In 1963, David McClelland founded McBer and Company as an outgrowth of his work in the department of psychology and social relations at Harvard. Its purpose is "to generate and apply scientific knowledge to practical problems of organizations in the optimum use of human resources"—how to use scientific knowledge to get people to do their best. Over the years, McClelland and McBer have worked with an amazing variety of organizations—major corporations (for example, AT&T, TRW, Kennecott, General Mills, Owens-Illinois, Honeywell, Rohm and Haas, Texas Instruments, Mattel); our government and its agencies (the army, navy, and State Department; the Peace Corps); foreign governments (Costa Rica, Ecuador, Ethiopia, Sri Lanka [Cey-lon], India); the U.S. Information Agency in Tunisia, Morocco, Spain, Mexico; and groups of small businessmen in various parts of the world, including a variety of minority communities in the U.S.A. In this work, McClelland and his colleagues made some interesting observations about achievement motivation and money, and achievement motivation and competition.

First, let's consider money. Many people believe that the main motive for getting things done well in our society is the de-sire to earn money, not the desire to do a good job. They think that to stimulate achievement is simple: offer to pay people well and teach them what to do. But the studies of achievers show that their main satisfaction in life is not money, but performing well. It's true that in general this means that achievers earn more money than non-achievers, but it's not their main interest, except that often it does provide definite, realistic positive feedback. It gives the message, "You did a good job."

In a typical large business, high achievers prefer to work in situations where they can feel, in themselves and by checking with evidence, that they are directly involved in making a better and better product and providing a better and better service. Or they may be volunteers in community projects, working to develop im-proved methods to solve problems and to improve specific aspects of community well-being—clean parks or streets, job programs, training courses, and so forth. They are not so likely to strive to be president or chief of an enterprise as they are to do a good job within the enterprise. Motivation tests of top executives of large businesses, for example, show that they are more power-oriented than achievement-oriented. This is not to say that the chiefs are not performing very useful services. The effective exercise of power to manage other people is vitally important. But their moti-vation is somewhat different, or becomes different, from achieve-ment motivation.

In families that raise high achievers, parents would not pay out allowance amounts according to what the children achieve and how well they achieve it. That makes them focus on the reward rather than on performing well. Allowances would be paid on the basis of need for the practical necessities of life and for some recreation. Good grades at school would be rewarded at home not by payment but by plenty of praise for a job well done, or for improvement over past performance. In fact, doing any good job—achieving challenging goals—is rewarded by praise for the job done, for the achievement, and by expressions of pleasure for good achievements, showing that you care, that you are pleased they have done well. Thus, achievement tends to become its own reward, and one achievement stimulates another without the extraneous motivation of money.

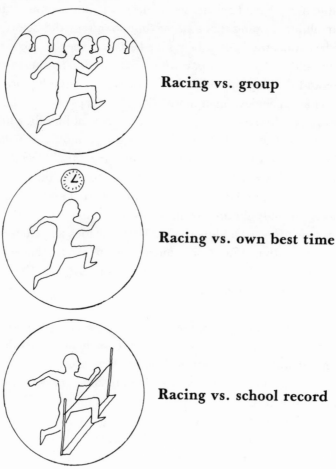

Racing vs. group

Racing vs. own best time

Racing vs. school record

■ *Achievers and Competition*

Many people believe also that competition, the desire to win, to come out ahead of others, is the main motivation for high achievement in our society. This is generally not so. To understand this, it is useful to recognize three kinds of competition. The most commonly recognized kind is *competition with others,* competition for the top place, competition to win. The studies show that this is not the kind of competition that mainly interests achievers.

Another kind of competition is *competition with one's own past performance.* You want to do better than you did last time, to know that you are improving. This kind of competition is important to achievers. They are less concerned about winning the race than about running it at a faster time than they did before. They are less concerned about being the best than they are about doing better and better. It's important for parents and teachers to recognize and develop this attitude if they want to develop achievers. It's a part of achievement motivation that keeps even people of not very great ability working to the best of the ability they have.

A third kind of competition, the one most likely to keep achievers motivated, is *competition against an internally held standard of excellence.* This means that the achievers hold in their minds an idea of what a good job is and strive to meet that standard of excellence. Not only do they want to do better than they have done, they reach toward a higher goal. This provides an achiever more satisfaction than praise or money. And it means that wherever achievers are, in whatever work situation, they can be counted upon to do a good job and to keep trying to do a better one.

In families that raise high achievers, parents tend not to emphasize competition with others, for in such situations there are always going to be winners and losers. Also, there are many situations in life where there are no others to compete with, or where such competition would be resented or inappropriate. The parents tend to emphasize competition with one's own past performance. Children are praised and their efforts approved when they do better than last time—when, for example, a boy is able to mow the lawn neatly and well in thirty-five minutes instead of an hour, and thus has time to do some weeding before he goes off to swim with his friends or gets a Popsicle and settles down to read a book.

Even more, families tend to emphasize competition with a standard of excellence and progress toward doing a very good job. It's not, "Great! You did that even better than Carlos," but rather, "Great! That's what I call a job well done! How did you figure it out so well?"

■ *Motivation Differences Between Girls and Women, Boys and Men*

For years, scientists and people who observe human behavior have noticed that the ways of thinking and acting of females tend to differ from those of males. McClelland, early in his work on motivation, said, "Men are rhinoceroses; women are contextual beings." By this he meant that boys and men tend to push right through to their goals, snouting aside or crushing whatever obstacles are in their way, whereas girls and women tend to be aware of the context as they act and move, and of the effects on others of what they do.

In men, achievement motivation tends to become mixed with power motivation; in women it tends to become mixed with affiliation motivation. Men tend to achieve because they enjoy feeling strong; women tend to achieve as they are aware that the achievement will have a good effect on others.

In a recent, very influential book, *In a Different Voice: Psychological Theory and Women's Development* (Cambridge, Mass.: Harvard University Press, 1982), educational psychologist Carol Gilligan points out, on the basis of some very convincing evidence from interviews, written statements, and observations of behavior, that women and girls tend to deal with the world differently from men and boys. Women move forward toward a goal with less ease and simplicity than do men. They tend to be less able to answer as quickly and clearly as men the question, "What is the right thing to do in this situation?"

Men, on the other hand, like rhinoceroses, tend to focus on

31

only one thing at a time, to see less. They are more concerned about abstract rules than are women. Since their motives and purposes are less affected by the effects on others, they have been seen by numerous psychologists and sociologists as able to be more directly effective in the world, as more powerful, as better achievers.

Gilligan's book reports evidence that boys tend to play competitive games more often than do girls and to play them longer. If there are disputes between sides, boys work them through and try to devise rules to settle things so that they can go ahead and win (or lose). But when disputes arise in girls' games, the girls tend to stop playing because they are more concerned with the relationships among the people involved than with completing the game.

Why this difference? One main reason is that most of the daily caretaking of young children is still done by mothers, not fathers. A young girl, cared for by her mother, can identify with her and enjoy being immersed in the world her mother, another female, lives in. But for a young boy an important task is to differentiate himself from his mother, to assert his maleness, his boyhood, so he learns very early to be a separate self. And, of course, these differences are reinforced by the way families treat girls and boys, the toys they provide, the ways they are physically handled, the ways they are spoken to.

One of the most important things that Gilligan shows is that women do tend to speak (and act) "in a different voice" from that of men. But another thing she shows is that our society has tended to value the male voice and way of thinking much more highly than the female voice. The most influential psychologists and social scientists, Freud, Erikson, Kohlberg, have tended to measure and judge human behavior by male criteria and to see female behavior as a deviation from the (male) norm. Freud called women "a dark continent." Gilligan points out that Piaget in his major work, *The Moral Judgment of the Child,* sees girls "as an aside, a curiosity." In Piaget's index there are four entries under "girl," none under "boy." Why? Because "the child," the subject of the book, is assumed to be a boy.

Gilligan does not say that the female voice is better or worse

Powmo

Affmo

Achmo

33

than the male voice, only that it is "a different voice," a vastly important one, and that this must be taken fully into account if we are to understand human life and motivation correctly.

Of course, it is important not to generalize too sweepingly about these different approaches to life. A good guess would be that perhaps a third of males tend to think in the "female voice," a third of females in the "male voice," with all sorts of gradations along the way and according to circumstances. Some women are "rhinoceroses" and some men are contextual beings.

As far as raising achieving children is concerned, you should be aware of the different "voices" in which your children express themselves and not push for a single road to achievement. We learn to set our goals, plan to achieve them, and work for them in ways I shall describe. Keep in mind that these ways are affected in our society by whether we are female or male.

■ *Putting It into Practice*

1. If you have a very young child (or know one in the neighborhood or in your extended family), observe his or her behavior closely and just notice—or jot down—examples of actions that seem to spring from one or another of the three social motivations:

> *achievement motivation:* the desire to do a good job and achieve a challenging goal (Example: building a tower of blocks)
>
> *affiliation motivation:* the desire to make friends and establish close, happy relationships with others (Example: hugging a person, climbing in a person's lap, smiling pleasingly)
>
> *power motivation:* the desire to feel strong and to control other people or things and to influence them (Example: using status, appearance, a firm look, a loud, peremptory voice to exert influence and control)

A parent with an older child will find it interesting to observe the baby's behavior together, making separate lists and then comparing them, or to talk about the baby's behavior as it happens.

2. Look back over the characteristics of achievers (pp. 24–27). Then in a family discussion, or a conversation between two members, or just for yourself, think of examples of the following taken from your own life or that of other family members:

a person setting a realistic, challenging goal

a person setting a goal way beyond his or her capacity to achieve

a person doing some good planning of what needs to be done to achieve a goal

some obstacles outside a person that have or had to be overcome to achieve a goal (world obstacles)

some obstacles within a person to be overcome if a goal is to be achieved (personal obstacles)

a person making good use of help in order to achieve a goal (the help can be from any source: books, magazines, experts, parents, siblings, teachers, etc.)

a person sticking at the job and achieving a goal even when strongly tempted by other desires or influenced by people or events to stop working

a person finding or inventing a better, more efficient way to achieve a goal or do a job than the way he or she had tried before.

3. Find examples of the same characteristics of achievers in TV programs, magazines, newspapers, or out in the community. Note them down, cut them out, or remember them, and talk about them in the family.

4. Years ago I took a course at Harvard in educational psychology. Our professor, O. Hobart Mowrer, showed us how to train rats in a special cage called a Skinner Box, after psychologist B. F. Skinner. When a hungry, untrained rat was put in the box, it roamed around at random until it happened to press a lever that released a food pellet into a dish. The rat smelled the pellet and ate it. After a few minutes, the rat learned that pressing the lever brought him a pellet and, thereafter, whenever he wanted food he

pressed the lever. He had learned that the lever brought the *reward* of food.

The bottom of the cage was made of small metal bars attached to an electric current. When the current was turned on, it was very uncomfortable for the rat. Eventually, after a lot of agitated movement, the rat bumped another lever, and the current went off. After a while, he learned to press the second lever to stop the *punishment,* the electric current. When two rats were put in the same box, they could be taught to stop the current in various ways. One was to stand absolutely still, since whenever they did that, the professor turned off the current. Another was to fight: after a while, in their agitation from the current, they would start to fight, and the instant they did the current was turned off. After a short time, as soon as the current went on, the rats would immediately fight for a second or two until the current went off. They had learned that fighting was the way to stop the punishment of the current.

This sort of learning is called *conditioning*. It works with children, too. Babies find that a smile gets a hug, so they learn to smile. A "Please" gets candy, so they say "Please." And so forth, into much more complicated behaviors.

Professor Mowrer said, semi-seriously, "No mother should be allowed to bring up a child till she has learned to train a rat."

Discuss with your family what you think Mowrer meant. Can you argue in favor of his statement?

Do you think that learning by conditioning, based mainly on reward and punishment, would succeed or fail as a method of raising children to achieve? Discuss the question.

5. Studies show that earning money is not the main motive for achievers. In fact, many people, volunteer workers, work very hard and well to achieve goals for which they are often, by choice, not paid.

Think of people you know about who are highly motivated to achieve without pay. What do they do? Why do they do it? Can you think of times when you yourself worked hard and well for nothing but the satisfaction of a job well done? Talk about these times.

6. Observe small children who are achieving goals because of competition, or discuss with older ones examples of achievement motivated by competition. Make a list of such activities under three headings: *competition with others; competition with one's own past performance; competition with a standard of excellence.* (See the illustration on page 29 to help make this exercise clear.)

Discuss examples of the three kinds of competition that you and your family find in magazines, newspapers, and stories, or see on TV.

7. On page 38 is a "picture" of nothing in particular, but in it a person can see all sorts of specific things and actions. Make three headings: *achievement, affiliation, power.* Under each heading list as many things and/or actions as you can see in the picture that in some way fit under one or more of the headings. Be prepared to explain why you put each item under the heading you did.

For example, in the picture I can see an ax hitting a man. I'd put *ax* under power. I can see the letter G shining light down on some place or person to make it feel good. I'd put *G* under affiliation. I can see a vine struggling to reach the top of the picture. I put *vine* under achievement. (You may see these things and dozens of others quite differently from the way I do.)

8. Choose some people you all know. Have each member of the family rate them either "high," "low" or "medium" on each of the three motivations: achievement, affiliation, and power. Discuss why you rated them as you did. Try to be specific about ways they act.

9. Here is a list of words related to achievement (or lack of it). Choose some of them to use three ways: in an affiliation motivation sentence, a power motivation sentence, and an achievement motivation sentence. You may add endings to the words to make your sentences work. (For example, for the word *adjust*: AFFILIATION MOTIVATION—"She always *adjusts* how she acts so that people will feel happy"; POWER MOTIVATION—"John is *adjusting* the TV so that everybody will be forced to watch and hear it";

ACHIEVEMENT MOTIVATION—''Alicia *adjusted* the engine so that it ran much more smoothly and efficiently.'')

accomplish	happiness
achievement	help
act	hinder
adjust	imagine
advice	imagining
anticipate	improve
awareness	initiative
better	knowledge
brainstorm	lie down
calculate	listen
challenge	long range
check	measure
commitment	obstacles
complete	patience
defeat	performance
define	persistence
disappointed	persuade
discouragement	plan
don't care	progress
efficient	proud
enjoyment	prudence
environment	realistic
evaluate	reality
excellence	research
experts	responsible
explore	rewards
fear of failure	satisfaction
feedback	seek
figure out	self-confidence
friendly	self-reliant
give	set goals
give up	short range
goal	standards

steady	try
step by step	want
strength	weakness
strengthen	win
strive	work
study	worst
task	worth
think	

10. Tell or write a story about achievement that includes twelve of the achievement words in the above list. In your story, have a person set a goal, plan to achieve it, work to carry out the plans, and succeed in achieving the goal.

PART II

A Six-Step Strategy for Developing Achievers

I n the 1970s an organization called Research for Better Schools, basing its work on that of McClelland, deCharms, and others, developed a six-step strategy for increasing the achievement motivation and skills of students in schools. This program was titled *Achievement Competence Training* (ACT).* These same six steps can be used by families who wish to raise achieving children. The steps are:

1. Study yourself.
2. Get goal ideas.
3. Set a goal.
4. Plan to achieve the goal.
5. Strive (work) to reach your goal.
6. Evaluate your performance.

Part II, the next six chapters, tells how you and your children can use these six steps to increase achievement motivation and learn the skills of achievement. Note that the steps are not separated into a strict 1 through 6 sequence (in real life). Accomplished achievers are frequently using the processes and skills in all of the steps as they work to reach the goals they set.

---

*The program was excellent, and careful studies showed it to be successful in many types of schools. But apparently because it involved tapes, tape-players, and games that were not easy for regular classroom teachers within a typical school system to use, ACT was never widely adopted by schools. In 1982–83, David McClelland and I, using ACT lessons and other materials we developed, wrote (and in 1984 Scott, Foresman published) what we think is a more workable program for schools, three workbooks, *Learning to Achieve,* for grades 4–7, 6–9, and 9–12.

3.

STEP 1.

STUDY YOURSELF

Achievers Think Realistically About Themselves

One of the main characteristics of achievers is that they keep in mind, insofar as they are able to, a *realistic* estimate of their strengths and weaknesses. The more that you are able to arrange life in and around the family so that the kids develop a sensible awareness of their own capacities, the better. It goes along with the realistic expectations I talked about in Chapter 1: challenging but possible expectations set at as early an age as appropriate.

I have heard parents say things to their children like, "You can do that if you just try a little harder," or, on the contrary, "It's no good your trying. You're pretty dumb. You'll never be able to do it." And there are parents who make the school's job much more difficult by claiming that their kid is a genius (and so if there is trouble it must be the fault of the school) or a general dope (and so nobody should expect much), when neither, in fact, is the case.

Parents, then, should try to hold a view of themselves based

45

on reality, and help their children to try, also. One good way to do this is in family conversations, or parent-and-child conversations. Let's imagine such a conversation, say, in the Smith family, with a mother who works part-time as a salesperson; a father who's an electrician; a daughter Amy, age ten, in fifth grade; and a son George, age thirteen, in eighth grade. The four of them are driving home after watching a basketball game. Note how the father and mother are encouraging the kids to think realistically about themselves.

GEORGE: Oh, darn it!

MOTHER: What's the matter?

GEORGE: I spent ten days trying to make this belt buckle and it just broke. I just can't do anything right!

MOTHER: Oh, George, it's just one thing. And the one you made for Amy is fine.

GEORGE: Yeah? And I got a D on my math test again. I'm just not good at anything.

AMY: Oh, you poor thing!

FATHER: Nobody can do everything, George, and it seems to me it makes a lot more sense to figure out what you're good at, not what you're not good at. Everybody feels the way you do sometimes, especially when they try something and it doesn't work.

MOTHER: There's some use to taking a good look at yourself, though, if you do it right. If we know where we're weakest, maybe we can work on that, and if we know our strong points, maybe we could use them more.

AMY: Oh, George is just fishing for compliments. He wants us to make a long list of all the great things he can do.

MOTHER: Amy! But you know, you've got an idea there; let's each make our own list. We've got a way to go yet, and there's a lot of traffic. Let's make it a game. Everybody has to say two things they're good at and two things they're not good at. How about it?

FATHER: Sounds intriguing. Kind of truth or consequences.

GEORGE: Well, it's better than memorizing license plates or counting cows.

AMY: I can't wait to hear what George is good at.

GEORGE: Yeah? Well I'm dying to find out what your star accomplishments are.

MOTHER: Come on, kids. George, you started this. Let's have yours.

GEORGE: O.K. Well, I'm good at buckles . . .

AMY: I'll go with that.

GEORGE: I haven't finished. Buckles and models and all kinds of crafts stuff. That's one. And I can swim laps like crazy. I swam more, faster, than any of the guys on the swimming team. But I'm not so hot at . . .

MOTHER: Good things first all the way around, then not good. O.K.? Dad?

FATHER: The driver is in the game too, huh? Well, I'm a good electrician. Thousands of satisfied customers will back me up on that. Well, if not thousands, all the ones I've had, anyhow. And I'm good at training other people to be electricians.

GEORGE: Isn't that the same thing?

MOTHER: No, it's not. Don't you know someone who's good at something and absolutely awful at teaching it to someone else?

AMY: You bet! My science teacher. All he does is . . .

Here, to save space, I'll simply report what the others said. Mother says she's good at organizing the hardware items they sell at the store where she works, and she can play any tune on the piano by ear. Amy says she's a red-hot speller and she can run faster than any boy in her class. The P. E. teacher told her she ought to go out for a regional elementary-school track championship.

Now let's take up the conversation again. There's still fifteen minutes' drive to get home.

FATHER: Well, it sounds as if we're all pretty good at some things. Now I've got—

47

GEORGE: Excuse me, Dad. Can I ask something first?

FATHER: Sure.

GEORGE: What about Aunt Selba? She's worked as a clerk or something in that warehouse for years, and then she just goes home and watches TV. And now the company that had the warehouse has moved out of the state, and she doesn't have a job any more. It seems to me she isn't much good at anything. She's not even married.

MOTHER: Wait a minute. Is it her fault she lost her job?

GEORGE: No, but . . .

MOTHER: She did very well at that job. She organized all their records. They thought a lot of her. I know that if she had wanted to move, they'd have been happy to have her go on working for them, but she didn't want to leave here. And do you know what she's doing now? She's got herself all organized to look for a new job. She's mailed out letters and references to about fifteen companies; she reads all the want ads and goes to see the places that have jobs she might fill. And just yesterday she got an offer, and she thinks she's going to accept it. She's good at getting on the ball and going after what she wants, so don't put her down!

GEORGE: O.K. I'm convinced. I guess you were right, Dad. It's kind of a balance, isn't it? Everybody is just better at some things than others.

MOTHER: And it always helps to sort out for yourself what they are. We're nearly home now. After supper, why don't we try looking at what we've set out to do and how well we've succeeded in it? Say two things we've brought off and two things that didn't work for us in the last two months.

AMY: O.K. But George has to say both kinds of things. I don't want to listen to a brag session.

GEORGE: Oh, yeah? One more word out of you, little sister, and I take that belt buckle back.

AMY: Oh, no! Please, sir, not that!

And so the members of the family, as part of their daily life, are learning to think realistically about themselves. The habit of having such conversations can spread from the family into the neighborhood and among groups of friends in surprising and varied ways. Now, of course I wrote this specific conversation to illustrate a point. In your family it probably wouldn't happen in just this way or quite so neatly, but it's worth figuring out ways to stimulate such talk. I don't mean, though, that parents should keep grimly, gravely trying to plot all the family talk to be the kind that will stimulate achievement motivation. That would be dull, and probably counterproductive, especially if most of the initiative came from the parents. But it is useful to keep in mind how children can learn, through family interactions and in one-on-one conversations, to think realistically about themselves, about their strengths and weaknesses, and about the goals they've set and achieved or not achieved. It is in ways like this that achievement thinking is developed.

■ Children's Literature and Achievement Thinking

I have emphasized, as does McClelland, the importance of how people *think* about themselves, other people, and the world, as a determiner of how people will act. Thought leads to action. Achievement thinking tends to lead to the actions of achieving. A remarkable confirmation of this idea is reported in *The Achieving Society*. McClelland theorized that the way a society thinks tends to be revealed in its stories for children. He writes:

> Such stories are simple, short and imaginative—at least in the sense that they normally do not yet deal with factual, historical events or political problems. They tell about imaginary situations, sometimes fantastic (from the world of fairies, giants, and dwarfs) and sometimes realistic (from everyday life), but the intent is everywhere the same—to provide something interesting and instructive for the child to read. In this sense the stories are "projective" and tend to reflect the motives and values of the culture in the way they are told or in their themes or plots. They are less likely to reflect external or historical events in the life of a nation, since children from the age of eight to ten are ordinarily considered not yet old enough to learn much about such things. They are given fiction instead.

Children's stories have many other advantages for our purpose. The same ones are read by nearly all school children of the same age, since textbooks are widely standardized in most countries. They represent therefore "popular culture"—what is considered proper for *all* children to read, not just those from a special social class. In this sense they should be less biased than novels, for example, which may reflect the motives and values of a much narrower segment of the population. Children's stories are also less subtle, more direct in their "message," than many other forms of literature. As Margaret Mead (1951) has put it so succinctly, a culture has to get its values across to its children in . . . [extremely] simple terms. Finally, and most importantly for our research design, children's readers, containing such brief comparable stories, could in fact be obtained from a generation ago for a representative sample of countries. The hypothesis could therefore be tested that achievement motivation levels in them would *predict* subsequent economic growth.

McClelland collected over 1300 children's stories from about forty countries all over the world. He chose them from two time periods: the years centering around 1925 and those around 1950, a generation later. He and his colleagues then analyzed the stories according to a definite code for images and actions of affiliation motivation, power motivation, and achievement motivation, and each story was given three scores.

When I was working on the achievement workbooks *Learning to Achieve,* I was allowed to look through the many file drawers at Harvard filled with coded stories. The collection is indeed impressive. The most impressive thing, though, is the results of the study. It turned out that to a highly significant extent those countries whose children's stories rated high on achievement motivation, thus revealing a high level of achievement thinking in the culture, tended to rate high in measures of economic activity. The *thinking* in the stories correlated with the *actions* of achievement in the country.

McClelland points out that the children's literature predicts economic activity. It takes time for a high achiever to start a business and show a gain in profits; and a nation's concerns, like a person's concerns, take time to show up in activities that are sparked by those concerns. So achievement thinking predicts gains in economic activity. You can tell ahead of time which countries are going to do well in economic activity, creating more and better paying jobs and providing more goods and services for their citizens.

Obviously, there are many other factors besides achievement thinking as revealed in stories that cause nations, and groups within nations, to prosper or not prosper (and the assumption that just because one thing *correlates* with another, it *causes* it, misleads social scientists into vast errors), but I think it can be said with confidence that McClelland's studies of children's stories and nations' economic productivity over periods of history do demonstrate the power of achievement thinking. (If you're interested in this topic, read Chapter 3 of *The Achieving Society,* "Achieving Societies in the Modern World." Then read Chapter 4, "Achieving Societies in the Past," to see how the same coding of folk tales, and even the images in paintings on vases, reveal and predict economic activity of certain nations during periods of their history.)

Now let's get back to our subject, how achievers think about themselves and how knowing this can help you raise children to achieve.

In Chapter 2, I listed the characteristics of achievement-motivated people. It's useful, too, to encourage your children to be aware of these, and to get them into their thinking. You don't say, "Now, be self-confident, or else!" or, "Dear, why aren't you better at dealing with personal and world obstacles? You'd *better* be!" But there are ways to help make kids aware of achievement characteristics: by example (probably accompanied by some explanation), or in conversation, reading, or TV-viewing. The "Putting It into Practice" at the end of this chapter gives some exercises that will be useful.

Also, there is another aspect of thinking in terms of achievement that a family might talk about when opportunities arise. Someone might raise the question: Can you think of a couple of times when you or others in the family were able to figure out better ways to do a job on something you were achieving but wanted to achieve better?

There's one additional idea that's important to emphasize at this point. Even though you may strongly desire to raise achieving children, or already have children who want to be achievers, you should never make success in achievement, or in developing the attitudes and characteristics of achievers, a condition that children must meet if they are to feel loved and supported by you. Your kids will be helped by the feeling, based on their experience, that you love and support them *as people* no matter what they do. You may be extremely critical, rejecting, or even forbidding of what they *do*, but you should try never to reject *them*, or make them feel rejected. "Hate the sin but not the sinner," the old saying goes.

■ *Putting It into Practice*

1. If you have a child between one and a half and three years old, think of various *expectations* you have held for that child since the age of one. List them in any order that you think of them, putting the age of the child when you first held the expectation. Then think about how each expectation worked out and beside each one write *realistic, too hard, too easy* (no challenge). What effect do you think each expectation had or has on the child's motivation for achievement? Discuss with someone you know well whether or not you hold realistic expectations for your child or children.

2. If you have older children, think back with them through their lives as far as they can remember. Together, list, or have the children list for themselves, the expectations you held. Beside each they should write *realistic, too hard,* or *too easy.*

Then discuss with them whether they came to accept the expectation as their own and made it their own goal.

3. If you can arrange it, have a conversation game session like that of the Smith family in this chapter. Remember, they each named two of their strengths and two of their weaknesses—such things as being good at crafts, making electrical things work, organizing items for sale; or being weak in math tests, spelling, basketball, keeping a tune. The point of the conversation is to encourage family members to be realistic about their strengths and weaknesses, one of the characteristics of achievers. In the conversation, it would be good, if there's any doubt about whether people are being realistic about each thing they mention, to have them give a specific example to prove it. Or perhaps your observation of another family can provide an example. If self-confidence seems to be a problem for members of the family, it will work better to mention only strengths so that people will tend to reinforce and encourage each other. Remember, though, the strengths must be real, not just made up to give false encouragement, which, in the long run, is likely to be discouraging when reality hits.

4. Perhaps each person, or some member of the family, would like to design a chart based on the specifics stated in number 3 above. This could lead to an achievement: a desire to strengthen weaknesses and especially to build on strengths and develop them.

5. Here is a rating scale for the characteristics that people who are highly motivated to achieve tend to have. On a separate sheet of paper, let all members of the family who'd like to do so rate themselves according to the given scale. After each rating, people should jot down or be ready to tell about a piece of evidence to back up the rating. When the ratings are done, it will be interesting for the family to discuss them with each other. (If you wish to duplicate this chart so that each member of the family may have one, permission is hereby granted.)

ratings Characteristics of achievers	I'm always like this.	I'm usually like this	I'm sometimes like this.	I'm seldom like this.	I'm never like this.
1. self-reliant and self-confident					
Evidence:					
2. realistic about my strengths and weaknesses					
Evidence:					
3. feel responsible for own activities; don't make excuses and blame others					
Evidence:					
4. set challenging but possible goals					
Evidence:					
5. plan carefully and intelligently					
Evidence:					
6. take personal obstacles into account					
Evidence:					
7. take world obstacles into account					
Evidence:					
8. know how to find and use help					
Evidence:					
9. keep working toward goals					
Evidence:					
10. check progress					
Evidence:					
11. like to achieve and dislike not achieving (imagine what it will be like to achieve or not to)					
Evidence:					
12. want to do a better job in better ways					
Evidence:					
13. use an achieved goal as a basis for new goals					

6. Here are three stories—fables from three different countries—that show high levels of achievement motivation. Read them together, and talk about how they show achievement thinking:

The Blind Man and the Lame Man (from Spain)

One day, a blind man and a lame man met each other.

"How much I should like to go to the city," exclaimed the lame man.

"I also should like to," said the blind man, "but I am afraid to leave these places with which I am familiar, for I might get lost. Since you can't walk and I can't see, we shall be able to help each other and carry out this trip to our mutual satisfaction."

"How can this be?" asked the lame man.

"Very simply," continued the blind man. "I shall carry you on my shoulders, and thus you will be able to walk with my feet, and you will guide me and explain what you see. I shall see with your eyes. In this way, I won't get lost, and I shall know where I am going."

Having hit upon this admirable idea, the two men put it into practice, and in this way, mutually helping each other, they arrived without stumbling where they both wished to go.

The Fox and the Armadillo (from Argentina)

One day, a fox and an armadillo made an agreement. The fox gave his farm to the armadillo to work, with the condition that they would split the profit.

As the armadillo is supposed to be a rather stupid creature, the fox thought he would trick him, and said, "This year, partner, I will take all that the plants yield above the ground, and you will take all that is below."

The armadillo agreed. But he was smart. That year he planted potatoes. He had a magnificent profit, and the fox had to content himself with useless leaves.

The next year, the fox said, "This year, I think it would be fair if I took what is below the ground, and you what is above it."

The armadillo agreed again, and he planted wheat, tricking the fox again.

55

The fox was very mad the next year because he had been tricked twice, and he said, "This time, I will get what is on the top and on the bottom, and you will get what is in the middle."

The armadillo said, "Fine, partner. You know I respect your opinion." And he planted corn.

When the harvest came, he got all the ears of corn, while the fox got all the top flowers and the roots.

The fox, trying to trick the armadillo, tricked himself into a bad bargain, and had to live in misery. This was his punishment for his slyness.

The Two Frogs (from Turkey)

Two frogs somehow fall into a container filled halfway with milk. Since the inside surface of the container is glazed and its mouth very high, the frogs cannot jump and get out, although they try very hard. So in order to remain above the surface of the milk, they start to swim. They swim constantly without stopping to rest.

A little later one of the frogs grows weary of this eternal swimming. He thinks that there is no solution to his problem, and he shrinks back. This state loosens his nerves and weakens his power. His feet don't move, his body becomes numb. It isn't long before the animal starts sinking. He goes to the bottom. He cannot come up again.

The other frog does not allow "dark thoughts" and fear to take over. Because he realizes that he will die if he doesn't move, he uses his breath and power sparingly, and he moves his feet incessantly.

After struggling for a long time in this manner, the animal notices to his amazement that the milk around his body slowly gets thicker and starts to solidify. This boosts his courage; he starts pushing his feet with more energy. At every pat of his feet the solid section increases, and a ball of butter is formed on the surface of the milk.

The frog immediately gets onto the butter and escapes death.

This is a very old story. But it can always serve as a good lesson for us. Because the first frog lets himself drift into dismal thoughts, he is left without hope; he becomes frightened and powerless and dies. The second frog does not give up hope because he keeps himself away from such dismal thoughts. Since he believes that struggle is better than death, he tries constantly and is saved in the end.

In life one meets many situations. It is necessary, even under the worst conditions, to keep hoping, never to bow before death, but to face it with a whole heart and, above all, to struggle to live. A person who can accomplish this can defeat even death and arrive at what he desires.

7. Write or give a character sketch of the most high-achieving person you know—or know of.

8. Describe a fictitious character, or someone in the public eye, and list five goals for that person. Rate each one on reality and challenge for that person. Now apply those same goals to yourself and rate them.

9. At the end of a week, make a list of what you did well that week. Answer the same question for another member of the family. Talk about your lists.

4.

STEP 2. GET GOAL IDEAS

Achievers Think about Their Goals:

They Have a Sense of the Future

A goal is something a person wants to achieve. Achievers are people who set goals and plan and strive to achieve them. People who set and strive for goals have a *sense of the future,* of wanting to move from where they are to where they'd like to be, and then to develop further goals and keep moving forward from achievement to achievement. People who have no goals, or for whom goals are not very important, tend to get stuck in the present and to settle for things as they are.

It is useful to encourage children (and parents, too) to think freely about goals and to consider all sorts of goal ideas, ideas for short-range goals and for long-range goals. This is achievement thinking. Many high achievers enjoy *brainstorming* about goals, either by themselves or with others. When you brainstorm, you just let your mind go free; you accept any ideas that occur to you for the moment and note them down, whether or not the goals are realistic and practical. Realism and practicality come later when, as an achiever, you *set* a goal and commit yourself to trying to achieve it. Brainstorming about goals, getting ideas for goals, is a good way to help develop a sense of the future.

As an example, let's take the same fifth-grade Amy of the family that in the last chapter was driving home from the basketball game. She reported two strengths: she spells excellently and can run fast. If there had been more time, she might have gone on to say that she was also good at writing stories and reports, and finding her way on a map. The weaknesses she would report were repairing things, cooking, speaking clearly to a group, and carrying a tune or singing on the note. If she'd been challenged to remember two past achievements, she might have told about cutting her time for running four circuits of the school playground track from seven minutes to six minutes in two weeks of trying. And there was the time last summer when she figured out from the road atlas the fastest route for the family to take when they drove to see some friends in another state. After checking it with her father, who made only one suggestion, the family drove the route in just about the time she had estimated, and everyone agreed it was a good route. As for goals she failed to achieve, she might report burning the eggs and toast when she set out to make a good breakfast for herself and two friends, and also the time she tried to fix an express wagon for some neighborhood kids and messed it up so badly that she had to help them buy a new one.

■ *Brainstorming for Goals and Then Judging Them*

Imagine that Amy had five minutes to brainstorm some *short-range* achievement goals for herself, goals she imagined achieving in the next week to six months. Here are some ideas that might come to her. (In a moment, I'll explain what the squares following each goal are for. Don't use them, though, until you get to "Putting It into Practice.")

Amy

Strengths	*Weaknesses*
Spelling	Repairing
Running	Cooking
Writing stories and reports	Speaking to groups
Using maps	Carrying a tune

---

1. Look for and find a million dollars
2. Get a job as tour guide to New Zealand
3. Write a detective story and get it published
4. Get an A in a story-writing unit at school
5. Cook gourmet meals for a restaurant
6. Borrow a quarter from Dad and buy some lemonade
7. Run a mile in ten minutes
8. Be appointed to make the announcements for all school assemblies
9. Hardboil an egg without burning it
10. Repair the wheels of baby brother's simple wooden toy
11. Sing a solo in a musical show
12. Double her allowance by vacuuming and washing supper dishes for Mom

Now, here are some ideas Amy brainstormed for *long-range* goals, goals that she imagined achieving by the time she was twenty-five years old.

1. Win the Olympic distance-running championship
2. Learn to cook well enough to feed a family of four
3. Become the chief editor of a well-known encyclopedia
4. Go into the travel business
5. Organize shuttle trips to Mars
6. Become the first woman president of the United States
7. Become a physical education teacher
8. Get a research job for a local TV news station

9. Jog three miles a day, five times a week
10. Develop an organization to keep world peace and stop all wars
11. Write and have published articles about physical fitness
12. Get married and bring up two kids

Can you think of any more long-range goals for Amy?

Having children brainstorm goals like this is one thing, and a useful one. Having them consider whether the goals they dream up are practical is another, also very useful. Deciding actually to set and strive for a goal, a medium-risk one, is still another, and I deal with that in the next chapter.

You noticed that after each brainstormed goal statement is an empty square. Those squares are for rating each goal for practicality: to what degree is each goal a practical one for Amy, given what you know about her strengths, weaknesses, achievements, and failures to achieve? You and your children, if they are old enough, will find it stimulates thinking about goals to rate each of Amy's goal ideas according to this scale:

1 utterly impractical
2 pretty nearly impossible
3 a big challenge that might be possible to achieve
4 quite easy to achieve with a bit of effort
5 so easy it's hardly worth calling a goal

For several of the goals there are no obviously right or wrong answers. It is good achievement training, however, to try to explain and defend the rating you and your children give each goal. It helps to get people thinking in future-oriented yet practical ways. "Putting It into Practice," number 2, suggests a method for doing this exercise, or you can just talk about it when an occasion arises in the family.

In order to stimulate your children and yourself to think about goals, I suggest that you keep alert to opportunities to discuss the goal ideas that different people have: people in the newspapers, on TV, in stories you read, in the family, at school, in the community. To what extent do people seem to be thinking about goals and getting goal ideas? It might be interesting to ask them. Can you think of examples of people considering short-range goals and long-range goals? Are there examples of people who set such far-out goals that they seem to have little connection with reality? Why do people think about goals like these? Are there people who seem to be without any goals—either ideas for goals or goals they have set?

■ Putting It into Practice

1. Babies and very young children aren't ready yet to think about the distant future but they can be stimulated in the achievement skill of looking forward and predicting. Here are two examples:

For twelve- to eighteen-month-olds:

Helping Her Predict

Adults can play a game that helps the child guess where an object might be after it's disappeared. The adult finds a *soft ball* and a *big box.* He stands with the child several feet from the box and throws the ball into it. He asks the child, "Where did it go? Do you see it?" If the child doesn't understand, he encourages her to look in the box. He lets the child be the one to "find" it and is very pleased and happy when she does. They again step away from the box, and the child is invited to throw the ball. Each time the adult acts surprised and pleased when the ball's found.

The game can be played another way with a *ball* and *tube.* The adult sits at one end and rolls the ball through the tube to the child and encourages the child to roll it back. She uses words such as "There it goes," "Here it comes," and "Through the tube."

When they play with the tube, the child may not at first expect the ball to come through. She'll try to look into the tube for it or pick up the tube to dump it out. After a few sessions she will start

63

to expect it to come out the other end. She is now anticipating what will happen because it's happened before.

The goal of the game is to give the child experience in predicting where an object will be that has gone out of sight. To help the child to expect things to happen.

For four-and-one-half to five-year-olds:

My History in Clothes

When one of the children asks what he or she was like as a baby, use this opening to stimulate some serious thought about the children's personal histories. A parent might say, "Let's look in this suitcase. I've kept some of your clothes in it that you've outgrown."

Let the clothes be a guide to discussing what each age was like. "See how the knees are worn on these overalls; you were still crawling when you wore them. And see, the legs of these can unsnap. That's because you weren't toilet-trained then." Conclude with a positive assurance about today. "You've grown so much. I like the age you are right now because we can do so many interesting things together that we couldn't do before." At another time you might remember with photographs or toys that have been saved.

This game helps children look forward by stimulating them to look into the past. They are helped to understand that they are undergoing tremendous growth toward the future.

2. Discuss the way you and your children have rated Amy's goal ideas on pp. 61–62 to help stimulate the children to think ahead freely and yet with some sense of reality.

3. Choose any object, preferably one that is broken, strange, or useless, and brainstorm all the uses that might be made of it. For example, here is a list of uses someone brainstormed in five minutes for an old, dented hubcap found in a gutter: dish, tray, trick frisbee, hat, protector for a hurt knee, picnic seat for a child on wet ground, shield for war of dwarves, birdbath, plant grower, something for a teacher to bang on to get the class's attention, pro-

tection against spanking to be worn under trousers, a Halloween mask (cut holes in it), half a scale.

Discuss the question: how might free brainstorming like this increase a person's achievement motivation?

4. It's fun and mind-stretching to play brainstorming games. It helps people get ideas for the future and to think about things in different ways, which can help strengthen achievement motivation, provided there is a good chance later to check the brainstorming against reality. This exercise can be done in writing or simply in discussion. I'll explain the writing way.

You and your children, or just the children if that seems better, jot down as many short-range and then long-range achievement goals for yourself as you can brainstorm, just the way Amy did. Remember, when you brainstorm, you let your mind go free; you don't trouble yourself with the question "Is it practical?" Short-range means in the next day to the next six months; long-range means, for a child, between now and age twenty-five, for you, the parent, perhaps between now and fifteen years from now.

After jotting, rate each goal on the same five-item scale you used for Amy's goals.

Then discuss your goals and their ratings, especially in terms of your own strengths and weaknesses and the real circumstances of your family and community.

5. Let members of the family make a list of six to twelve short-range goals and six to twelve long-range goals that each one might *realistically* set and strive to achieve. They are not necessarily actually setting the goals and committing themselves to strive for them. These are still only goal ideas, not goals that are set.

Discuss the lists that are made.

6. People sometimes ask themselves: What shall I do with my life? What do I want to be? What field of activity do I want to go into? Over the next few days, as you read books, magazines, and newspapers, as you watch TV, or as you hear people talking, note down specific examples of real people or characters in stories who are considering these questions. In each case, write down (or remember) the name or identity of the person, the person's age, and

the ambition that the person stated or thought about. Later compare notes and discuss your findings.

7. This is a prediction exercise. Use those parts of it that are appropriate to the age of the people who are doing it.

In an individual conversation, or one with a group, help people to have a sense of the future by asking questions like these:

What is the next thing that is going to happen right here with us?

What will happen ten to fifteen minutes from now?

What things will happen between now and the time you go to bed tonight?

What things will happen, do you think, during the next week? How about the next month?

Predict how things will be different for you/us a year from now.

Predict for ten years from now.

This game can be fun just as informal, mildly guided conversation at table or in the living room or car, or it can be more organized, with someone jotting down answers. If you jot down answers, then you can go back over them and put the further question: What goals may you have to set and achieve in order to cope well with what you or others predict?

8. In the family, use whatever opportunities you find arising naturally to discuss the question: Why do some people seem to have no long-range goals? It will be more useful if you talk about specific people. Be careful not to put any family member on the spot so that he or she feels threatened. However, some members may welcome the opportunity to discuss the question in a non-challenging sort of way, and this can be a way of stimulating achievement thinking in people and thus increasing their motivation to achieve.

9. What does this quotation from Antoine de St. Exupéry mean: "The convict's stroke [of the pick] is not the same as the prospector's"? What has it to do with achievement motivation and goals?

5.

STEP 3.

SET A GOAL

Achievers Set Challenging Goals

A major difference between high achievers and other people is that *achievers know how to set goals for themselves that are challenging but, with effective effort, possible.* These are called *medium-risk goals.* Risk does not mean danger or luck. It means a challenging possibility of succeeding or not succeeding depending mainly on how well you plan, calculate, and strive—do your best.

■ *The Ring Toss Game*

In scientists' study of goal-setting behavior, a by-now classic game is Ring Toss. McClelland made much use of it in his studies and research. The object of the game is to win a payment by tossing two of four rings onto a peg. In a common form of the game, the players have to decide how far from the peg they wish to stand: three, six, nine, twelve, fifteen, eighteen, or twenty-one feet away. At three feet, it is obvious to the players that it's almost impossible not to make two out of four ringers. There's no challenge. It is also obvious that from twenty-one feet only a superhuman could toss two ringers unless there were some lucky miracle. The task is practically impossible.

Another element of the game is that players receive payments for making two out of four ringers. Typically, a player must "invest" 10¢ for the right to play. (You can use jelly beans or some other tokens if you don't approve of playing for money.) The payoffs for tossing two out of four ringers are: 10¢ at three feet; 25¢ at six feet; 40¢ at nine feet; $1.00 at twelve feet; $2.50 at fifteen feet; $4.00 at eighteen feet; and $10.00 at twenty-one feet. Scientists found, both for five- and six-year-old children and, in similar separate experiments, for college students, that people who were known by other experimental evidence to have high achievement motivation tended to behave in certain ways:

They examined and thought over the situation carefully to calculate the chances of making two out of four ringers.

They then chose to stand a middle distance from the peg, say nine, twelve, or fifteen feet, so that it would be a challenging goal to toss two ringers, but not impossible, and the payoff would be good, 40¢ to $2.50.

But people with low achievement motivation, both children

and college students, much more frequently stood either very close to the peg so they couldn't miss or get paid much, or at eighteen or twenty-one feet, where only a stroke of luck, not skill, would get them two ringers and a big payment.

Another element that high achievers valued was an opportunity to try out the game in advance to see by experience what the reality of the risks was—how difficult the game, how great their skill. Then they would use these facts as a basis for their decision about how far away to stand. Achievers enjoy calculating the risks, the probabilities of achieving goals before they set them, and they try to take real facts and experience into account as they figure the chances. If they don't have any actual experience, they use their imaginations to try to create as realistically as possible an experience on which to base their decisions. "Hmm. Now, let me see. How will it work?" would be a typical achiever attitude.

In general, scientists have found in various experiments in risk-taking to achieve a goal, that high achievers choose a goal that they calculate they have about a 30 to 50 percent chance of achieving. In *The Achieving Society* [p. 212], McClelland describes the situation among Ring Toss players thus: "If they stand close to the peg, they are much more likely to throw the ring on . . ., but they are less likely to get any feelings of achievement satisfaction from doing so. If they stand too far away, they are both much less likely to succeed and more likely to regard success as 'luck' than if they stand at a moderate distance. . . . In fact, they are behaving like the businessman who acts neither traditionally (no risk) nor like a gambler (extreme risk), but who chooses to operate in a way in which he is most likely to get achievement satisfaction (moderate risk)."

In "Putting It into Practice," your children and you will have a chance actually to set up and play the Ring Toss game as an exercise in goal-setting.

■ *Definite and Measurable Goals with a Time Limit*
In Chapter 1, I explained that children can increase their achievement motivation by choosing goals on their own, as with

the McClelland boys' goal to save enough money to buy a TV set. The satisfaction of setting the goal for yourself, working toward it, and achieving it because of your own effective efforts simply feels good. It's rewarding, you enjoy it, and therefore you want to do more of it. So *a characteristic of achievers' goals is that they are chosen by the achievers themselves,* or, if they are imposed by others, the achievers find ways of making them their own. (How they can do this I explain in Chapter 9, "How Achievers Deal with Goals and Rules Imposed by Others.")

Two other characteristics of achievers' goals are that *they are definite enough so that the achiever knows when he or she has achieved the goal,* and that *they have a time limit to aim for, either a length of time or a date.* These characteristics are especially true of short-range goals, somewhat less true of long-range goals having to do with plans and goals for a person's lifetime objectives.

Examples of short-range goals that are not definite enough to satisfy an achiever might be: learn to play a guitar; make a model car collection; try out for the lacrosse team; make better use of time around the house; do an ecology project; bake some things to eat. Achievers would tend to make these more specific, thus: borrow a guitar and master the first ten lessons in the book so that our guitar-expert neighbor will say, "O.K., you're ready for more advanced work;" collect twenty-five model cars, all made of metal, not plastic; earn position of center on the junior high school lacrosse team or, if that's too hard, wing position; finish six assigned household chores on Saturday to Mom's satisfaction by 10:00 A.M.; get five or six people organized to keep the shrubs and flowers in one corner of the park watered, clipped, and weeded; bake two dozen chocolate cupcakes that the family will say are good to eat. Notice how specific these achievers' goals are.

Achievers tend to try to set a definite time or date for accomplishing, or learning to achieve, their goals: do all that with the guitar before Thanksgiving; collect all those model cars in time for the hobby show on February 25; and so forth.

Good ways to let children develop a sense of satisfaction in achievement is to encourage them to make their goals definite.

71

You could ask a question like, "What do you mean, do your chores better and faster?" Another is to make it a point to report feedback: "Hey! Jill really got that park project going in two weeks. When I was sitting in the park yesterday I heard two people I didn't know say, 'This looks great! Look, no weeds, and those bushes are so well trimmed.' "

■ *Setting an Actual Short-Range Goal*

In the "Putting It into Practice" at the end of this chapter, there is an exercise that gives members of your family an opportunity to set a short-range goal for themselves, that is, actually to do Achievement Step 3. At the end of the chapters that follow, a "Putting It into Practice" exercise will continue the process, using Steps 4 (plan), 5 (strive), and 6 (evaluate) to carry the same goal through an entire achievement process. Before we get to that, I'll describe a specific example. We'll use 13-year-old George of the Smith family, about whom you first read in Chapter 3. As you go through George's thinking and activities for achievement, it may be helpful to refer to the four characteristics of an achiever's short-range goal:

1. It is a *medium-risk* goal. It is challenging to achieve, but possible. It is not easy; it requires your best effort.

2. It is a goal you *choose yourself*. It is not set *for* you or forced on you. You take responsibility for it.

3. It is a *clear and plain* goal. You can know definitely whether you have achieved it.

4. It is a goal with a *time limit*. It can be achieved by a certain date, or within a certain time period.

Recall some initial facts about George. A part of his going through Step 1, *Study yourself*, revealed that among his strengths were crafts and "making things" and swimming laps fast. We need not take space to list some of his weaknesses, his past achievements, and goals he failed to achieve. Thinking about these would also be a part of Step 1. Nor need we specify the goals that George brainstormed as a part of Step 2, *Get goal ideas*. You, the reader, can imagine those as you wish. Now we come to

George and Step 3: *Set a goal*. He decides he wants to achieve something definite in the area of crafts, which his self-study and past achievements show he's pretty good at. Let's listen to George thinking to himself:

"I really enjoy doing crafts things like leather and pottery and carpentry. The family still uses those mugs and saucers I made for us back in fifth grade, and I sure find the bookshelves useful that I built for my room last year. I really enjoy doing a good job on things like that. Let's see, what could I make that the family would like? I know; I'll ask them." So he does and finds that his mother would love to have six more coffee mugs; his father would like a really nice IN-and-OUT box to hang near the front door to provide a place where the family can put the mail when it arrives (IN) and a place for outgoing mail (OUT). Amy says she'd like to have a little wooden box of drawers to keep her paper clips, tags, thumbtacks, staples, and other "desk junk" in so they won't get lost, "if it's not too hard to make."

"Well, O.K.," George goes on thinking, "I'm pretty sure I can make all those things, even Amy's desk box." He ponders the time he'll need and thinks, "I know what. I'll set my goal to make the thing each person wants in time for their next birthday. That'll be Dad first; for December 10—his IN/OUT box," and he goes upstairs and marks "Dad's in/out" on his calendar for December 3, a week in advance, "in case anything goes wrong." "And February 8 for the mugs for Mom—gee, 'Mugs for Mom!'; that'd make a good name for a crafts company," and he checks February 1 for Mom. "And May 17 for Amy's desk box," May 10 checked on calendar.

"O.K., that's it. I've set my goal. Maybe if I can get all that done well I'll have enough experience to start a store or summer business or something," he thinks. "But first I've got a lot to do." Almost at once, like an achiever, George starts thinking about what he'll need to accomplish his three-part goal. But that gets us into planning, Step 4, which is in the next chapter.

■ *Putting It into Practice*

1. Play the Ring Toss game with members of your family. If there are those too young to play, let them watch and help as they can or just play parts of the game. The game is explained on pages 67–70. If you can't get or make a peg and a ring, use a small box as a target and a ball to toss into it. Use masking tape to mark off the distances on the floor. Write the number of feet on each strip of tape. The payment scheme, remember, is as shown on this chart:

distance	payment
3'	10¢
6'	25¢
9'	40¢
12'	$1.00
15'	$2.50
18'	$4.00
21'	$10.00

In most cases, it will be better to use fake money made of cardboard coins and imitation paper dollars. Or you can modify the payment amounts and use jelly beans or M & M's.

Play the game three times, once by yourself, once with the whole group watching, and once with the group watching and for actual payment. The third time you have to pay an agreed-on amount to play.

Keep a record of each person's performance on a sheet or large piece of cardboard, like this:

NAME	RING TOSS RECORD		
	Round I (alone)	Round II (people watching)	Round III (for pay)
Juan			
Mom			
Maria			

2. Discuss these questions about playing the Ring Toss game:

a. How did you decide what goal to set each time you played the game: alone; with people watching; for "pay."

b. Did you make your goal each time? Why or why not?

c. A characteristic of achievers is to figure better and better ways to do things. Did you figure any better ways to set goals and earn payments as you played the game? Explain and compare your methods with others.

d. People who are highly motivated to achieve tend to set medium-risk goals. Did the way you and members of your family played the game show this statement is true or not? Explain.

e. Can you think of other situations in your life or the lives of your family in which you set medium-risk goals? Tell what they are. Discuss how the goals were set and what the results were.

3. Another goal-setting game scientists have often used to study how people set goals and to train them to set goals so as to be better achievers is the game of *Scrambled Words*. Here are two scrambled words. See if members of the family who may be playing the game can unscramble them:

LAMBDERCS SDOWR

If you figured it right, you saw or figured that the words were "SCRAMBLED" and "WORDS."

The game requires you to choose which of the following five groups of five words you think you can unscramble in three minutes. (For most people, group 1 (three-letter words) is quite easy; group 5 (seven-letter words) is very hard. If you can unscramble all five words in three minutes you score as follows: Group 1, 15 points, Group 2, 20 points, Group 3, 30 points, Group 4, 45 points, Group 5, 60 points. But if you can't finish *all* the words in the group in three minutes, your score is zero.

Your object is to score as high as you can. You have to set your goal in advance: which group you will strive to unscramble.

Below are the five groups for Round I of the game. Someone who is not going to play the game should copy the five groups in big letters on large sheets of paper, one set on each, each set numbered. Then you glance for not more than ten seconds at the five groups and then cover the page and, after thinking, set your goal: Group 1, 2, 3, 4, or 5. Write your goal on a separate sheet of paper: Group number and score.

In a moment you'll be ready to play the game. Some person who's not playing will be the timer, saying "GO!" at the start and "Stop!" at the end of three minutes.

Before anybody starts playing, it's probably worth reminding everyone that the purpose of this game is just to show how people set goals, not to have a great big competition. Later, though, with groups of scrambled words you can make up for yourselves, it can be fun to set goals and really compete, either against your own past record or against other players.

Now you're probably ready to have people play the game. Put the word group rectangles where everyone can see them, and start when the timer says GO! Then turn to page 80 to get the answers, if you need them.

GROUP 1. Three-letter words

THA

UNF

BOR

AMJ

EPI

Score 15 if you unscramble them all in three minutes.

Group 2. Four-letter words (Score: 20)

ROYU

INPA

ROPO

PLCA

OSOZ

Group 3. Five-letter words (Score: 30)

TAFIN

SRAHH

DOBOL

YLEJL

SKYIR

Group 4. Six-letter words (Score: 45)

ERUDEC

TYPTER

SKRNID

ODLEON

LAMRON

Group 5. Seven-letter words (Score: 60)

TRELTAP

CUMLASI

GAPESAS

STECKAR

BOOTCAC

When the timer says *Stop!*, all the players put their pencils down. Then you can figure out the right answers for the groups people set as goals and see how each person scored—either zero if there was a mistake or the person didn't finish, or the score given for the group that was completed correctly.

After the game, talk about the following questions:

a. Did you achieve your goal? If not, why not?

b. If you did, do you think you could have set a higher goal? Why?

c. If you played the game again but with different words, do you think you could score higher? Why? Did you learn any unscrambling tricks?

If you'd like to play the game again, here are five more sets of words, the same length, difficulty, and scores. Copy them on large sheets of paper if several people are to play. (You will find the answers on page 80.)

Group 1: YOB, OTO, TEP, OPP, ANC
Group 2: EROT, SMOS, ERTE, AWTI, MWIS
Group 3: REVEN, ATING, THOGS, ULDOA, LOVEW
Group 4: SOPREN, TRYLAP, HOTREM, WHENEP, VICETA
Group 5: LETRUST, MAGNISU, TRETTSU, NENLACU, YELLGAR

The family may enjoy this game. If so, make up your own scrambled-word groups, and go to it. The practice will help people set moderate-risk goals and figure better ways of unscrambling, as well as stimulating the use of language—all things that can increase achievement motivation.

Note: If you have young children who are just beginning to learn to write, they can share in the fun of this game by doing very simple unscrambles, like PU, EM, TUO, NI, OG, YOB, LIRG, and EES. Remember that when you scramble a word for a game, it may be unscramblable in more than one way. (However, this is not the case for the scrambled words in the groups given above. Each is unscramblable in only one way.)

4. It may be that members of your family play video games in arcades or on your TV set. These games can be used as strong teachers of medium-risk goal-setting. Players can set their goals based on (1) their past performance; (2) the performance of others with whom they are playing; and (3) with a standard of excellent

performance known for a given game. Such goal-setting, probably already done by many players, requires achiever-like calcula-
tions, achieverlike thought and practice to figure out new and better techniques to raise one's score, and sometimes persistence
(which in arcades is expensive!).

Talking about video games and the achievement attitudes
and skills involved in playing them well can help young people
transfer the attitudes and skills over into productive aspects of life,
in school, on the job, in the community.

5. If members of your family old enough to do it are already
eagerly setting medium-risk goals and working skillfully to
achieve them, the following exercise will not be needed, even
though it may provide interest and encouragement. For less-
achieving members, it can make the process of setting, planning
for, striving for, and achieving goals more real.

Find a time when there is an opportunity to talk together for
a little while without any feeling of pressure or compulsion. Look
back over the account of how thirteen-year-old George Smith set a
challenging short-range goal: to make certain birthday presents
for the members of his family on or before their birthday dates.
Then have each family member consider and actually set a short-
range goal, a goal which they commit themselves to strive to
achieve. To be sure it's clear, have each member write the goal on
a sheet of paper. (For those too young to write well, let someone
else write the goal down for the goal-setter.)

Does the goal each person sets have these characteristics:
medium-risk? chosen by self? clear and plain? time limit?

When each of you has your goal written down, you have
completed Achievement Step 3, Set a Goal. Explain that for this
goal it would be interesting and probably fun to wait until you've
done the exercises in the next chapters, on planning (Step 4),
striving (Step 5), and evaluating (Step 6), before going ahead.
However, many young achievers will be so gung-ho to get at it
that they will not want—or even be able—to wait. Good! Let
them go. There's nothing good to be taught by your commanding, in effect, "Now don't you start achieving till I give permis-

sion!'' If your achievers get the goal achieved before you get to later chapters and exercises, no problem! Another goal can be set for the material in the next chapter.

For very young children, say from two to four or five, this exercise is probably too abstract, but you can encourage youngsters as you see them going through the steps to achieve goals by praising the job they are doing and (in moderation) verbalizing for them the process they are going through. (Examples: ''That's going to be hard to do, but I bet you're going to be able to do it.'' ''Great, that's real progress!'' ''How much longer do you have, do you think? Do you need longer?'' ''It's great when you figure out what you want to do.'')

(*Note:* At one point, on page 73, George saw a business opportunity in a part of his goal. It would be interesting to see if anyone noticed it, and then to discuss whether any of the goals people have set show any promise, maybe much later, of becoming a productive money-making enterprise.)

6. Write a high- or low-risk goal, and then make it medium-risk for yourself, for someone else you know, for a character in a book, television program or for a figure in the news.

Answers to Scrambled Words:

Game 1:
  hat, fun, rob, jam, pie
  your, pain, poor, clap, zoos
  faint, harsh, blood, jelly, risky
  reduce, pretty, drinks, noodle, normal
  prattle, musical, passage, stacker, tobacco

Game 2:
  boy, too, pet, pop, can
  tore, moss, tree, wait, swim
  never, giant, ghost, aloud, vowel
  person, paltry, mother, nephew, active
  turtles, amusing, stutter, unclean, regally

6.

STEP 4.

PLAN

Achievers Plan Effectively to Reach Their Goals

Once achievers set a goal, they do not simply ride off madly in all directions trying to achieve it. They *plan* what tasks they need to do to reach the goal and in what order to do them. They consider what resources and help they may need. They think about any obstacles that may stand in their way, obstacles within themselves, obstacles outside themselves, and how they can deal with them. Here is a specific report from an achievement motivation project:

> After having had training in Achievement Motivation at his school, Sean told his teacher that putting tasks in order was especially helpful. He illustrated this by telling about a model rocket he had built at home. Before starting work on it, he had made a list of all the steps he would have to go through and then had gone over the list to see what he should do first. Sean had become conscious of planning as a self-initiated and self-directed activity, as compared to the way he had worked previously, when planning was something accidentally engaged in.

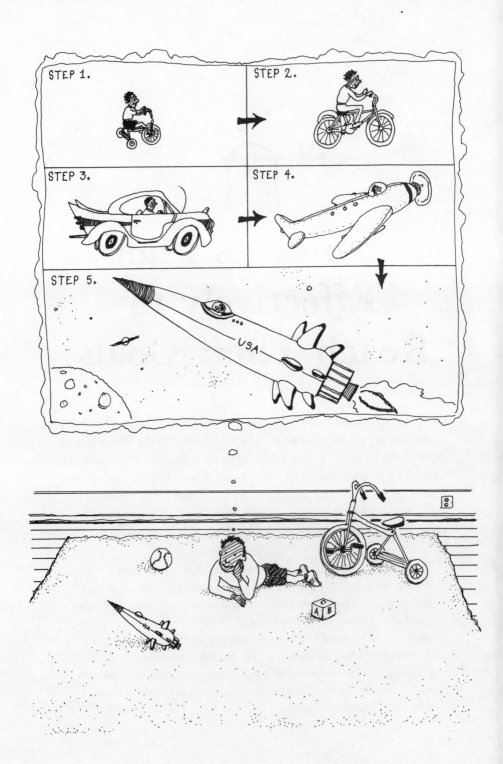

As your children set and work toward their various goals, you can help them learn the skills of planning by discussing their plans with them, occasionally suggesting planning ideas they might use, and by praising them for their efforts when they seem promising. It is important, though, not to do the planning *for* them. If they are to feel and enjoy the satisfactions that come from setting goals, planning for them, and achieving them, the actual work must be theirs. From these satisfactions and joys come strenghened motivation to achieve more and more.

I emphasize that children must be given ample opportunity to accomplish the steps of achievement on their own so that they can become responsibly independent. Anita Shreve makes the point very well in an article in *Parade Magazine*, "Why I Do Not Want My Child to Be Too Secure" [*Parade Magazine*, August 14, 1983, p. 13, *Boston Globe*]. She tells an experience she had with her two-year-old daughter. A two-year-old is too young to do much systematic, conscious planning, but little children do engage in lots of gut-level planning, planning that leads to growth and independence. Anita Shreve writes:

It is the first good afternoon of spring, and I am out in the backyard with my two-year-old daughter. . . . Katherine, after five months of winter confinement, is dizzy with the need to run and explore. . . . My daughter heads straight for the one part of the yard I was hoping she'd ignore: a three-foot-high stone wall that separates our yard from our neighbor's.

There are about sixteen reasons why I wish she was not attracted to that stone wall. She *could* lose her grip as she learns for the first time how to find footholds in the rocks. She *could* fall and break a tooth if she lands on a hard stone. . . . My impulse is to guide her to her fenced-in play yard. . . .

But I don't.

Although I am perched nervously at the end of my chair, with talons ready to snatch up my baby bird at the first sign of faltering, I let her go. . . . She has caught sight of a watering can on the other side and wants to touch it. She grabs the top rocks and finds, in a tentative yet eager way, her path up the stone wall. The going is tough, but she is determined. Once her little leather-soled shoe slips from a rock, but she hangs on with surprising tenacity and does not complain when she scrapes a finger. . . . I watch her mount the summit and turn toward me with an air of triumph not even Lindbergh could have matched. "I dood it!" she crows with a shiver of delight.

■ *Listing Tasks and Putting Them in Order*

A skill achievers develop and use once they have set a goal is that of figuring out just what tasks they'll have to do to achieve it. They may be able to figure out the tasks in their heads and then arrange them in some sensible order without writing anything down, or it may help to jot down an informal list for planning and arranging. They may be helped in all of this by talking with others about what they need to do and what comes before what. It's good for family members to be available for such talk, for listening, reacting, occasionally advising, often encouraging.

Again, let's take thirteen-year-old George Smith as an example. What are the tasks he'll have to accomplish in order to achieve his three-part goal of birthday presents: six coffee mugs for his mother; an IN/OUT mailbox for his father; and a wooden desk-box for his sister Amy? Here's how he might jot them down at first:

Tasks to Do

1. Draw actual plans for IN/OUT and desk-box
2. Be sure I've got necessary tools for woodwork (borrow neighbor's power jigsaw and routing tool?)
3. Get materials for wood items
4. Find secret place to hide stuff while making
5. About mugs, arrange for time in school pottery room and with kiln
6. Find out secretly exactly what sort of mugs Mom wants
7. Same for IN/OUT and desk-box
8. Work out exact schedule to get things done (but O.K. if ahead of schedule)

9. Ask Mr. Hersh, shop teacher, for advice after plans are drawn

10. Get boxes and birthday wrappings

11. Write a note or poem for each present?

12. Figure if I've got enough money to buy the stuff I'll need

13. Ask Dad if I can use his basement shop at special times when nobody's there

14. Go over this list with Kevin to see if he thinks of anything I've forgotten

A good exercise would be to read over these tasks and try to arrange them in a logical order. It might make the subject of a conversation, or any member of the family could do it alone. It seems fairly obvious that the first tasks to be done would be the ones now numbered 6 and 7, and the last probably number 11. ("Putting It into Practice," number 1, gives a practical way to do this exercise.)

■ Getting Needed Help

High achievers are generally quite independent people who like to set their own goals and work for them. But they are also realists who know that they can't do everything themselves, that they need to learn, and that they may need help. One of the things they are good at is recognizing when they need help and figuring out how and where to get it. For instance, George Smith recognized that to make the birthday presents for his family he'd probably need help from the teacher in charge of the pottery room, from a neighbor for certain tools, from the shop teacher for construction advice, from his dad to be allowed to use the basement shop tools, and from his friend Kevin to check over his list of tasks. Notice that the kinds of help George planned for were the sort that would strengthen him and his abilities, not weaken them. He didn't ask the pottery teacher actually to make the mugs, nor did he ask Kevin, "Now, what will I have to do?" He asked for assistance or advice that would help make George a better, stronger achiever both this time and in the future.

It's important at home that you as a parent not be so ready to help that you end up doing too much for your children, thus making them more dependent, less independent. Try not to be the sort of achievement-squelcher who says, in effect, "No, not that way. Here, let me do it for you so it'll be done right." It's much better to say, "How about trying this way to [do whatever it is]?"; then, if necessary, show or teach the child and say, "O.K., want to try it?" It's like the old Chinese saying, "Give a man a fish and you feed him for a day. Teach him to fish, and you feed him for life." That is, he can feed *himself* for life.

Parents (or teachers) who explain too much too soon, or a parent, say, who holds or protects her exploring baby too much (as Anita Shreve was tempted to do with two-year-old Katherine), may retard their children's progress as achievers. Children need to be allowed to make mistakes, to keep trying. Vernon Law, a champion pitcher for the Pittsburgh Pirates in the 1950s and 1960s, said after he had retired, "Experience is a hard teacher because she gives the test first and the lesson afterwards." If you let your children make some mistakes and learn from them, and give only the help that strengthens, rather than trying to teach everything before the children experience it, you are more likely to raise achievers.

One of the best things I ever saw in a school was in an eighth-grade classroom. At the front, above the chalkboard, and printed in large letters, was a sign reading: "IT IS SAFE TO MAKE A MISTAKE IN THIS ROOM." Excellent, I thought. And the sign continued, in slightly smaller letters, "BUT MORE TO YOUR CREDIT TO MAKE A DIFFERENT ONE EACH TIME."

Another teacher, Abbie G. Hall, wrote in 1891 about the "management" of a one-room school, "Every thing that is explained to a pupil that he can find out for himself robs him of so much education." And of course Abbie Hall included girls in that "he", as well as boys.

The more you as a parent can maintain a climate of high expectations and help that strengthens, with freedom for children to plan and strive and make mistakes, and to learn from them, the better.

■ Figuring Out the Obstacles and What to Do About Them

When a person tries to achieve almost any medium-risk goal, there will be difficulties and obstacles in the way. Sometimes all that is needed to overcome them is the ability to keep working hard. In the next chapter, I'll suggest ways that children (and adults) can develop their striving skills. But very often simply plugging away isn't enough, and it may not be an intelligent way to deal with obstacles. Usually, it's better to plan: to figure out what the obstacles will be and how to overcome them or get around them. Remember, obstacles tend to fall in one of two categories: those within the achiever, *personal obstacles,* and those outside the achiever, *world obstacles.* For example, let's go back to ten-year-old Amy Smith. In Chapter 4, one of the short-range goals she brainstormed for herself was, "Double allowance by vacuuming and washing supper dishes for Mom." Let's suppose she decided to set this as her goal. Here's a list of some obstacles she might meet. As you read and discuss them, decide which ones you think would be personal obstacles and which world obstacles.

1. Mother seems to enjoy washing the dishes herself and talking with people while she does it.

2. Amy is careless with machinery and has twice broken the vacuum cleaner cord when helping clean the house.

3. Amy has friends who call her on the phone in the early evening, and she can't make herself not talk to them even though there are other things she should be doing.

4. There is a family rule that right after supper is homework time, no matter what.

5. George might want the money, too, and would argue that he should get the jobs because he's older.

6. Amy tends to be forgetful and might not remember to do the agreed-upon jobs when she's scheduled to do them.

As you and your children consider these obstacles, can you agree which are personal ones and which are world ones? Discuss any difference of opinion you might have. Can you think of ways Amy might go about overcoming the obstacles? What specific suggestions do you and your children have? "Putting It into Practice" provides a chance to try to answer these questions.

It can happen that obstacles to achieving goals are so great that they cannot be overcome. Good achievement planners learn to recognize that fact and to deal with it in one of two ways: They give up their goal as impossible instead of struggling against insurmountable problems, or they modify their goal so that the obstacles become more manageable.

Sometimes obstacles seem greater to less-motivated, less-skilled people than to others. An example would be the situation where a hesitant driver, waiting for traffic to clear, came to a complete stop on the ramp entering the freeway where there was a YIELD sign. At last the traffic thinned, but the intimidated driver still waited. Finally, a vigorous voice yelled from behind, "The sign says to yield, not to give up!"

■ *Putting It into Practice*

1. On pp. 84–85 is a list of fourteen tasks George Smith figured he'd need to do to achieve his birthday-present goal. Look at the list and try to decide on a sensible planning order for the tasks and list them in that order. A good way to start is to decide on which tasks need to be done first, and which might be done last. Then fit the others in between. No single order is best, but you should be able to explain why you put each step where you did. It will make the job easier if you jot down the tasks on a sheet of paper in shortened form: 1. (#8) work out schedule, etc. Be sure you discuss with one another how you arranged the tasks.

2. Look at the list of obstacles Amy Smith might face in working toward her goal of doubling her allowance by vacuuming and dishwashing. Discuss and decide whether each one is a *personal* obstacles or a *world* obstacle.

Are any of Amy's obstacles likely to be so great that she

should give up her goal? If you were Amy's best friend, how would you advise her to cope with each obstacle?

3. Consider by yourself or with members of the family the following matters about the place of help in the achievement of goals.

A. Think of a goal where *you* needed help to achieve it and the help really *did* help and also strengthened you as an achiever. Then think of an example for another person, perhaps a very young child whom you observed.

B. Think of a situation when you set a goal and were planning and working for it, and then you got too much help or someone even seemed to take over the job and do it for you. How did you feel? Think of the same situation for another person you observed, again possibly a very young child.

C. Think of an example of where someone actually butted in when you were working to achieve a goal and you resented it. How did it turn out? Have you seen this happening with a person you observed?

D. Can you think of an example when you were allowed to make a mistake and learned from it? Explain. Do you agree that "we learn from our mistakes"? Should people ever be allowed to make a mistake when someone near them could show them how to avoid the mistake?

4. If you can get the opportunity, carefully observe a child between six months and two years of age dealing with obstacles and take notes (or watch with someone else and compare observations while you watch). Do the same with a two to four-year-old and a five to seven-year-old. What signs of achievement motivation (if any) did you observe in each? If you have a camera and can do so without being noticed too much, take pictures showing the overcoming of obstacles or being defeated by an obstacle. Or perhaps you'd rather draw pictures.

5. Discuss at some time what you think Abbie Hall meant when she wrote, "Every thing that is explained to a pupil that he can find out for himself robs him of so much education." Do you agree with Miss Hall?

What about the sign, "IT IS SAFE TO MAKE A MIS-

TAKE IN THIS CLASSROOM, BUT MORE TO YOUR CREDIT TO
MAKE A DIFFERENT ONE EACH TIME.'' What does it mean? Do you
agree with it? Could the same thing be said about the house you
live in? Is it "safe to make a mistake" in this house? Explain.

6. Believe it or not, many deaf and learning-impaired people
now have furry, barking tail-wagging ears! The idea was first developed in the 1970s by the SPCA in Minnesota. The goal: to provide Hearing Ear Dogs, who could be trained to hear for their
masters and mistresses somewhat as Seeing Eye Dogs see for
theirs.

Imagine that you or your family have set as your goal making
a plan for this service. Before reading further, write down in a list
all of the skills you can think of that you'd have to teach the dog in
order to achieve the goal. Write your list now; then read on.

Now read the following account of how the actual project
works at the SPCA in San Francisco, using the dog Penny as an
example. As you read, write a list of the skills Penny was taught
and compare that list with the one you made. How good a job did
you do in foreseeing what needed to be taught?

Penny the Pup—a Dog Learns How
to Hear for People Who Can't

The dogs chosen to be trained in the Hearing Dog Program
are strays or abandoned animals that have been brought to the
SPCA. Most are mixed breeds, usually small or medium size,
since large dogs can be difficult to care for in an apartment or small
home.

Every few days a trainer checks the animals available for
adoption. She looks for dogs that are friendly, alert and curious. A
young dog, between six months and two years, is generally the best
candidate. A dog this age takes well to training and can look forward to a long life with its new owner.

A dog that seems promising is given a thorough medical ex-
amination. Special attention is paid to the ears. A good sense of
hearing is vital for a hearing ear dog.

If the new dog is healthy, and if the trainer feels it has the right temperament for hearing ear work, it is admitted to the program.

Training begins with basic obedience lessons. Penny learns to come when called, to walk obediently on a leash, and to sit, stay and lie down on command. Hand signals, as well as voice signals, are used because some deaf people have trouble speaking.

When basic obedience lessons have been successfully completed, Penny begins training for her new job.

Since hearing ear dogs work primarily in homes, they need to be trained in a homelike setting. At the San Francisco SPCA, an entire apartment—complete with kitchen, bathroom and bedroom—has been set up. There is even a family cat on hand to get the dog used to household pets.

A special machine reproduces common household sounds. Using a hand-held remote control device, the trainer can set these sounds off in various parts of the apartment. She can make a telephone or doorbell ring, as well as trigger an alarm clock or smoke alarm.

Penny learns basic responses to household sounds. In the case of an alarm clock ringing or a smoke alarm sounding while the owner is asleep, she is taught to jump on the owner and wake him up. The trainer teaches the dog to do this by lying down, setting off the alarm and calling the dog. When the dog comes, the trainer gives it plenty of praise and a small treat, which she holds in her lips. Sometimes, a trainer pretends that she is asleep. She doesn't give the dog its treat until the dog has worked hard to wake her up.

Other situations call for the dog to run back and forth between its owner and the source of the sound. When the doorbell rings, for example, the dog must run to the door, then back to its owner, until the owner realizes someone is at the door.

Hearing-impaired people can sometimes use telephones with special amplifiers built in. The hearing ear dog is trained to tell its owner when the phone rings. At the San Francisco SPCA, trainers place a treat near the phone. The dog-in-training collects its reward when it runs to the ringing phone.

Dogs can be trained to respond to other sounds as well: a baby crying, an oven timer ringing. People who want hearing ear dogs apply to the SPCA, and list their specific needs. The trainers can use tape recordings of these sounds to teach the dogs to meet these needs.

Training a hearing ear dog takes about four months. At the end of this period, the new owner comes to the SPCA. Now it is his turn to be trained.

The first step is getting acquainted. Then, Penny and her owner practice together. The new owner must learn what to expect of Penny. He must learn how to praise her for working well. And he must learn how to keep up her training.

This last step is especially important, since once a dog is in its new home, training can easily be disturbed. For instance, if another member of the household sometimes answers the door or the telephone, the dog may give up responding to those sounds.

The Hearing Dog Program at the San Francisco SPCA is funded entirely by donations. It costs about $2,500 to train a dog like Penny, but deaf and hearing-impaired people receive the dogs free. The trainer and the new owner keep in touch. If there are problems, the trainer helps solve them.

Sometimes dogs go beyond their training. In households with babies, dogs have learned to tell the difference between a normal cry and a cry of distress. Some have saved their owners' lives by alerting them to gas leaks and fires. When a trainer hears such stories, she knows that the time and energy put into a Hearing Dog Program are well spent.

7. Sometimes when achievers plan the steps to reach their goals, new information or considerations arise and they have to decide whether or not they have to *re-plan*. Sometimes if they don't re-plan, they will fail. Sometimes the new facts do not require re-planning. Achievers are good at calculating when they need to re-plan and when not. The game ''Seven Cities of Gold'' gives you a chance to exercise your judgment about re-planning. You play it by looking at the map on pp. 94–95. You are one of several Spanish explorers in South America in 1685. You are searching for the fabled Seven Cities of Gold. You begin your journey down the River-of-No-Return, through vast equatorial jungles. By a trick of history, you are able to make your journey in canoes that are

motor-powered and have very high sides. (Keep these and other facts in mind.) Also, you have radio communication with the outside world. It will bring you some new information as you proceed with your trip.

The best answers to each question are given on page 96. Don't look at them until you have finished the game.

A. All right, look at the map. What is the shortest route from San Goalo to the Seven Cities? Write it down. Mention the cities (each marked with a large black dot •) and geographical features you will pass, such as Mirror Lake.

B. Just before you come to Mirror Lake you hear some new information by radio. Heavy rains have caused the water to rise three feet. Make a judgment: Will you have to re-plan your route? If so, what change in your route will you make? Tell the route.

C. At San Gusto the radio informs you that between there and San Giorgio the river is overrun with hundreds of fierce alligators. They can attack even large boats, overturn them, and eat the occupants. Will you re-plan? If so, how? Tell the route.

D. You are now on your way to Fort Garbanzo, the alligators having caused you to change your route. You hear terrifying news: Fort Garbanzo has been taken over by fierce jungle tribes who use poison-tipped spears and arrows. If a person is even nicked by a spear or arrow, that person dies in thirty seconds. The tribes have sworn that no intruders will be allowed to pass the fort. Will you re-plan? If so, what will be your route?

E. At San Giorgio you learn that near the Seven Cities the River-of-No-Return is filled with piranha—small, fierce fish that eat anything with flesh that is in the water. They can strip a pig to the bones in three minutes. Will you re-plan? If so, how? Remember your facts.

F. Now, look up the answers and see how you did. Did you reach your goal (and the gold!) by the most efficient way? If yes, congratulations! If not, what miscalculations did you make?

G. If you'd like to, make up a few more pieces of information that might have been received by radio, present them to someone, and ask for a judgment about re-planning. Compare your judge-

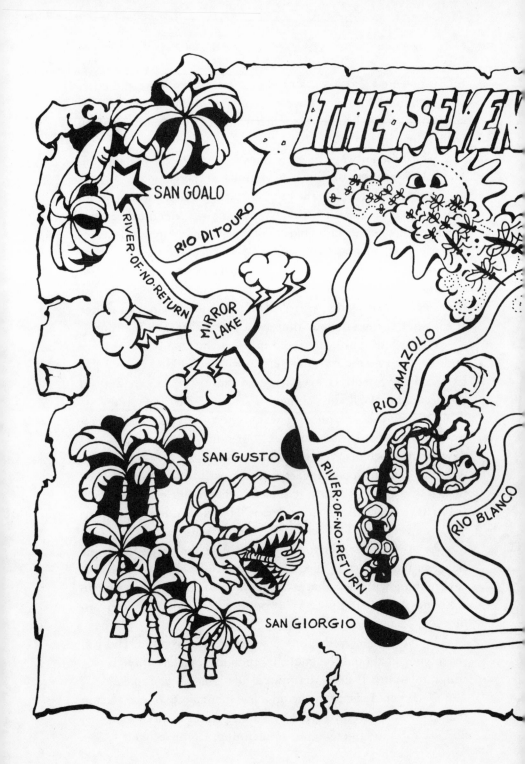

STOP!

ment with that of the other person. Of, if you're more ambitious, make up a new fantasy journey, with a map or diagrams and various dangers or obstacles that might require re-planning, and give your game to others to play.

Answers to Cities of Gold Game Questions

A. Shortest route: San Goalo down River-of-No-Return, passing Mirror Lake, San Gusto, San Giorgio, and on to the Seven Cities.

B. Re-planning of the route via Rio Ditouro is not efficient. Three feet of water pose no danger.

C. The danger is too great. Re-plan. New route should be up the Rio Amagolo to Porto Fino, past San Paulo and Fort Garbanzo, and then to Seven Cities.

D. Danger is real. Re-planning is needed. Go back to Porto Fino. Take Rio Blanco to San Giorgio and then on down the River-of-No-Return.

E. No re-planning needed. Your canoes have high sides. If you stay in the boat and don't dangle your hands or feet in the water, you're safe.

8. Remember the goals that people in your family set at the end of the last chapter. Take out the paper on which you wrote your goal, and do your planning to achieve it. Write down the plans as best you can or discuss them with others and get them written down. Your plans will probably include:

a set of tasks to be accomplished

arranging the tasks in order

stating any obstacles—world obstacles and personal obstacles—you may need to overcome and how you plan to do it

stating any help you may need and where you plan to obtain it

figuring out whether your goal and your plans to achieve it are *responsible*—that is, good and not harmful for you and others, both now and in the future

If, because you are a strong achiever, you have already achieved your goal, great! Think back and discuss the plans you made to achieve it and how they worked out. Then *set another goal,* write it down, and do the planning for it, using whatever is useful that you have learned from this chapter. In the next chapter, you will be asked to *strive* (Achievement Step 5) to achieve this goal.

9. Talk or write about obstacles that have stood in your way as you worked toward a goal (or are standing in your way right at present). Tell how you overcame them, or plan to overcome them, or whether you must re-plan because of them. Include both personal obstacles and world obstacles—those within you and those in the world outside you.

7.

STEP 5. STRIVE

Achievers Develop Striving Methods: *Ways to Keep Working toward Their Goals*

Two people famous for getting a lot done are Joseph F. Kennedy, father of former President John Kennedy, and auto manufacturer Henry Ford. Kennedy once said, as a maxim for his sons, "When the going gets tough the tough get going." Ford said, "Nothing is particularly hard if you divide it into small jobs."

   Obviously, most people, no matter how highly motivated to achieve, are not going to become father of the President of the United States or spectacularly successful industrialists. Obviously, too, both Kennedy and Ford were motivated not just by the desire to achieve, but also by power—the desire to be influential, to make an impact. But their words do remind us that achievers don't give up easily and don't overwhelm themselves trying to do everything all at once.

■ Some Striving Methods

Not all high achievers are the same, and they develop their own ways to keep progressing toward their goals. Here are ten methods many achievers use. The first four are relatively mechanical systems, like Henry Ford's idea. The last six have more to do with how achievers think.

Here are the four striving systems:

1. *Achievers divide their tasks into manageable pieces so that they are aware of progress.* For example, if your daughter decided to put new washers on the spigots in the house, after getting the needed advice and learning the needed skills, she might break up the job into several parts: buy the equipment needed; do a couple of spigots and test them to be sure they work; then do the others one or two at a time each Saturday morning before going out to do other things. Or if your son had lines to memorize for a part in a play, he might learn three pages a day, or one scene a day, with periodic reviews, so that the job would be done in time.

2. *Achievers set aside specific times to work.* For example, if a boy has a reading list to get through by a certain date, he might decide to read every evening for an hour after supper, or for three-quarters of an hour before going to sleep, or after waking up (by alarm clock), no matter what.

3. *Achievers keep going on hard tasks by promising themselves a reward after a certain period of work.* For example, if the goal is to keep a part of the park weeded, watered, and clipped, the achievers might promise themselves: "O.K., after we work steadily for an hour, we'll take a break and have some lemonade and cookies"— but not until a solid hour of work is done.

4. *Achievers keep energized by making a checklist of tasks to be done and marking them off as they are accomplished.* This is a way for people to organize their own feedback. They can see (and almost feel) their progress. For example, if the goal is to put on a party for a team and its opponents after the last game, a checklist of refresh-

ments needed, cups and spoons, tables, ice, volunteers to serve, etc., etc., can help give a realistic sense of progress.

And here are six striving methods that have to do with achievement thinking:

1. *Achievers are encouraged by remembering their own past achievements.* They strengthen their image of themselves as achieving people. For example, if it's clear that it would be useful for a second grader to collect all her own equipment (clothing, lunch, books, etc.) and be out and ready for the school bus and a girl sets that as a goal, at first she may be discouraged when she forgets things. But if she remembers, or is encouragingly reminded by a parent or sibling, that she succeeded in collecting her stuff for summer day camp, she gets a new burst of energy.

Sue found that when she thought of her past achievements as a horseback rider, she would get an idea of how to solve a problem she was currently having. By thinking of what she had accomplished in the past, she gained confidence that she could solve the problem she now had.

2. *Achievers are stimulated to keep striving by a sense of competition,* especially competition with a standard of excellence or with their own past performance. They are moved to keep trying by their sense of wanting to do a good job, or a better job. For example, in a daycare center, or at home playing with others, toddlers see other toddlers making it across the room on two feet, using no hands, squealing with delight, and they struggle harder to do as well; a girl who wants to play the trumpet with an orchestra is inspired to more practice by hearing a recording of a famous trumpeter, which provides her with a standard of excellence.

3. *Achievers imagine how good they will feel when they have achieved their goal.* They picture in their minds that race well run, that piece well played, that meal deliciously cooked, or that tower of blocks built as high as the table, and this vivid idea of the rewards of achievement stimulate them to further effort.

4. *Achievers imagine how bad they will feel if they don't achieve their*

goal. Again, imagination and a sense of the future help to keep them striving. For example, a boy who has determined to learn ten poems for school so that he can recite any of them to the class may be spurred on by feeling in advance how unhappy he will be if he doesn't do a good job, if he doesn't achieve his goal.

5. *Achievers seek and get encouraging pep talks from experts they respect in the field in which they are striving.* For example, if your six-year-old son has decided to set it as his job to make the hallway by the front door clean and neat every day, and he's becoming discouraged by his inability to get all the mud off the rug, you, the expert, can say (only if it's true!) that it *is* a hard job, and the rug looks a lot better than it did, and look what a great job he's done on the rest of the hallway, and with a little more practice and maybe a wet rag for the worst spots, he'll really have learned the job well.

6. *Achievers are kept going by thinking about people they know or read about or see on TV who are "achievement heroes" in the field in which they have set their goals—achievers they admire.* For example, an achieving father or mother or sibling can be an inspiration to a child who is trying to keep at work toward the goal. But the striving achiever must be allowed to think of the "hero" pretty much on his or her own, not have it drummed into him or her: "Your father (or mother) gets such great [whatever it is], so why can't you!" Much of that kind of pressure is likely to be a turn-off.

■ Some Catchy Words

Three American authors wrote some interesting words about striving. Mark Twain remarked, "Don't go around saying the world owes you a living. The world owes you nothing. It was here first." In other words, *you*'ve got to do it!

An editor and verse-writer, Frank L. Stanton, wrote:

> *'Taint no use to sit and whine*
> *'Cause the fish ain't on your line;*
> *Bait your hook and 'keep on tryin',*
>   *Keep a-goin'!*

And Henry Wadsworth Longfellow wrote:

> *Let us then be up and doing,*
> *With a heart for any fate;*
> *Still achieving, still pursuing,*
> *Learn to labor and to wait!*

Perhaps a member of the family would like to print up boldly and place in a conspicuous spot in the house one or two of these sayings, for the minor inspiration of achievement in the family.

■ *Teaching Children to Use Striving Methods*

There's no doubt that the best way to keep striving is simply to feel that you *want to;* in other words, to be motivated to achieve. But the more your children strive and achieve and feel the satisfactions of striving toward achievement, the more strongly motivated they will become. As you see your children setting goals, small or large, short-range or long-range, you can, if it seems helpful, encourage and empower them by suggesting some of the striving methods you've just read about. And as you do this, other members of the family may develop the habit and learn to be aware of when someone in the house can use a striving method. It might even be that a striving-method poster around the house would be a stimulus (see "Putting It into Practice," pp. 88–90).

For example, let's take thirteen-year-old George Smith and his birthday present project. Suppose his mother had learned about the desk-top box he was making for Amy.

GEORGE: (coming up from the cellar where he's been working, and grumbling in a discouraged voice): I just can't do it well enough. It's too hard a job to make it look decent so Amy'll really like it.

MRS. SMITH: You mean Amy's box? Well, that's just like you to want to do a good job. Want me to look at it?

GEORGE: Well, OK, sure.

So Mrs. Smith goes down into the cellar with George and finds that while the desk box isn't going to be a masterpiece of American handicraft, it really looks quite good. The dialogue might continue:

MRS. SMITH: George, that looks great to me! I know Amy'll like it.

GEORGE: But look at the way the drawers don't fit in perfectly evenly.

MRS. SMITH: You're right, they don't. (She pushes the drawers in and out.) But they work all right, and they'll do the job for Amy. I like the design and the shape.

GEORGE: Yeah, that looks OK, I guess.

MRS. SMITH: Well, you know at the hardware store I like organizing things for sale. All I can say is that this box is going to be great for Amy to organize her desk stuff in.

GEORGE: But what about those uneven drawers?

MRS. SMITH: Frankly, I don't think Amy will notice them, she'll be so glad to get the box. Wait till you see her face! And a craftsman like you knows how much a little sanding can improve things.

GEORGE: But the time. It's tough getting enough time to finish this thing.

MRS. SMITH: Sometimes I have that trouble. Don't we all! Except for people who don't care. Sometimes I find it works just to set aside half a day or a day, not answer the phone, and do nothing but a project I've got to do. Could that work for you?

GEORGE: Hey, great! I'm just going to cancel everything for next Saturday, go down in the basement with some sandwiches and soda, and *work!* I bet I can finish the box.

Notice that in the conversation Mrs. Smith leaves George plenty of space to make his own decisions; she's realistically encouraging; she helps George think about how great he'll feel when he succeeds; she gives suggestions but not orders, one about sandpaper, one about use of time. The chances are George comes out of this talk more strongly motivated to achieve and with a better knowledge of striving methods. Ask yourself what strengths that George has that she recognizes and gives him feedback on? Look back over the conversation and see.

The same sorts of talks together work well with children from two or three years old right through until the time they leave home. In fact, they work well with a spouse or even with yourself.

■ *Putting It into Practice*

1. Go back to page 99 and reread the quotations from Henry Ford and Joseph Kennedy. Discuss what you think Henry Ford means. Do you agree with him? Which striving method is he describing?

What does Joseph Kennedy mean? Is this a good motto for achievers?

2. If there are members of your family who like to draw, suggest that it might be interesting to make a poster or a series of pictures titled STRIVING METHODS. Discuss the posters or pictures and put them up somewhere to stimulate people to think about how to keep working toward their goals. Another possibility is to draw a picture and see if everyone can agree on which striving method it is supposed to illustrate.

3. In a family discussion, or by yourself, think of times when you used one or more of the ten striving methods described in the chapter. What was your goal? What was the method? Did the method help you?

4. Psychologists who studied achievers found that they tend to cheat somewhat more than people who are unmotivated. How would you explain this? The fact that an urge to achieve causes some people to cheat has caused some authorities, especially in schools, to say that, therefore, we should try to remove competition from schools. Which do you think is preferable: to remove competition so that there is no reason to cheat, because there's nothing to win or to strive for, or to try to teach people how to strive and compete honestly? Explain your answers and discuss them.

5. It is clear that one thing that encourages people to keep striving to achieve good goals is positive feedback—not "You're great!" but "That's great, what you did!" As a family, try to recall examples of positive feedback, or just by yourself try to recall times when you provided someone else with feedback or when you received it from someone else. How did giving or receiving feedback make you feel? Also, try to remember: Was the feedback based on facts or was it just made up to provide encouragement? Which type is better? Why?

6. In 1955 a psychologist did an experiment to see whether Air Force officer candidates who were highly motivated to achieve behaved differently in a coding exercise from those who were not achievers. (She knew by other tests which people actually were high achievers.) The exercise required the players to use a code that showed which numbers went with certain letters (A = 1, B = 37, C = 6, D = 16, E = 3, etc.). The Air Force men were required to put the correct number under each of a long series of letters. To one group of subjects, the test was introduced casually: "We are just experimenting today and we appreciate your cooperation very much. We want to find out what kind of scores people make on these tests." To a second group, the test was introduced in a serious manner: "We are measuring a critical ability, the ability to deal quickly and accurately with unfamiliar material. It is related to intelligence and to your future career." The third group was told: "The five men who make the best scores in five minutes will be allowed to leave right away. The others will have more practice periods and more tests." Which of these introductions do you think appealed to the people who most wanted to perform best? Why? Think out your answer before you read on. (The answer is that the first introduction appealed most to men who wanted to please others; the second to men who wanted to achieve; the third to men who wanted to escape from work and to rest. The second group, the achievement motivated men, did best on the test. Discuss why you think this was so.) Can you think of any reason why a high achiever might have been appealed to by the third introduction?

7. An interesting game that is used to study people's behavior and help them understand what situations cause them to strive best is the Tangled-String Game. Try it out with members of the family who are interested, or any of you can do it alone. As we use the game here, it will be mainly to show those who play it what kind of competition motivates them most strongly, competition with *a standard of excellence,* with *others,* or with *your own past performance.* The game involves working with a picture of some balloons that have gone up in the air but have gotten their strings all mixed up. The object of the game is to follow the strings and discover which balloon string is being held by which holder. You can follow the strings with a long, pointed object like a knitting needle or a mechanical pencil with no lead. (You don't want to mark the picture.) Then, on a separate sheet of paper, you write in a circle the letter or number of the balloon being held by each holder. To get the idea, and without making any marks on the page, try the very easy sample, game Number 1 on page 109. Have someone time you. If you are over eight years old, twenty seconds would be a good, normal time to be able to do Game 1. Some people will be a little faster, some a lot slower. If you got a wrong answer, then you failed to achieve your goal and need to figure ways to be more accurate next time. You get no "credit" for partly correct answers!

To practice again, try Game 2, on page 110. To complete Game 2, thirty seconds would be a good, normal time.

Now we come to Games A, B, and C, on pages 111–113. They are all differently tangled, but they have been tested and all present just about the same degree of difficulty—that is, they each take the same amount of time to complete.

First you will play Game A. You are competing with a known standard of excellence, thus:

    **** excellent time: one minute, forty-five seconds
    *** very good time: two minutes
    ** good time: two minutes, thirty seconds
    * fair to poor time: three minutes or over

Now play the game with someone to time you. Did you get each balloon attached to its right holder? (The answers are on page 119.) What standard were you able to reach: four-star, three-star, two-star or one-star? Make a note of your time.

Now, or when you're rested, play Game B. This time you'll be competing with other people, possibly some members of your family, or maybe some friends. You'll play the game one after another if you have only one copy. (If you wish to duplicate this page or the other tangled-string pages, the publisher hereby grants permission. In that case, you can all play at the same time and write your answers and time on the game sheet.) When you've finished, see how you did compared to others. Be sure to check your answers with the correct ones on p. 119.

Now play Game C. This time you're competing against your own past performance to see if you can do a better job, as achievers want to do. When you've finished, after checking the correctness of your answers, compare your times. Did you improve?

Now answer for yourself or discuss with others these questions:

Which striving method caused you to work hardest: competition with excellence; with others; or with your own past performance? Explain. How did you feel while you played each game?

Did you develop any techniques for doing a more accurate, faster job as you played? Share with the other people what they were. If your time was better on Game C than on Game A, was it better methods of playing that caused the improvement or different kinds of competition? Explain and share your feelings about this.

What way is there that might enable you to cut your time by about one fourth? What risk is involved in using this method? Did you take the risk? If you did, did it ever cause you to get a wrong answer? If you were to play the game again, would you take this calculated risk? Explain.

Game 1

Game 2

A B C   A B C   A B C

Game A

A B C D   A B C D   A B C D   A B C D

Game B

A B C D   A B C D   A B C D   A B C D

Game C

ABCD   ABCD   ABCD   ABCD

8. If you have very young children who get interested in the Tangled-String game, let them try it with Games 1 and 2. For a three- or four-year-old a good time on Game 1 would be thirty seconds if someone else writes down the answer. For Game 2, forty-five seconds would be a good score. If young children want to try the challenge of Games A, B, and C, by all means encourage them to. That shows they're ambitious to try harder goals.

9. You can make a very interesting goal-setting game out of tangled strings. Draw (yourself or someone else), say, five games, from very easy to very hard. Then have the players choose which game they figure would be a medium-risk goal (challenging but not impossible) for them to set, knowing that they are limited to forty-five seconds. Either they get all the balloons correctly attached to their holders or they fail their goal. As a model for how to set up the game, see the Scrambled-Words game you played. It's on pages 75–78.

10. In Philadelphia, the Fidelity Bank, out of concern to serve the community and to encourage people, and especially minority people, to achieve, annually distributes *The Afro-American Historical Calendar,* each month giving a brief illustrated account of the life of a successful black person. Here are four of these accounts, slightly shortened, each of which can be used as a case study in goal-setting and striving. Read them and then discuss what evidence there is in each of *successful striving*—working toward a challenging goal.

Some questions to discuss are:

a. What goals did the person set during his or her life? Mention long-range and short-range goals.

b. What obstacles did the person have to overcome? How did the person overcome these obstacles?

c. A characteristic of achievers is that they do not use "the system"—obstacles out in the world—as an excuse for their failure to achieve. They are determined to "pull themselves up by their own bootstraps." They feel that "if I don't help myself, no one is going to do it for me." This has been especially true of minority groups in America. The obstacles have been real—and are

114

real today—but high achievers just work all the harder to over-come them. In each story below, what excuses might the person have used to try to justify not making an effort to achieve goals?

d. On the other hand, encouragement and help from others can strengthen achievers. Are there examples in the stories of the person using really needed help to strengthen efforts to reach goals?

e. Can you, parents and children, think of times when you blamed the system and thus didn't strive as hard as you might have done to achieve your goals?

Rebecca Lee (1833– ?), first American-born black woman physician
Rebecca Lee was born in Richmond, Virginia in 1833. It is known that she excelled at elementary school there, but little else is known about her early life due to the destruction of many city records during the Battle of Richmond in the closing days of the Civil War.

Lee's lifelong ambition was to become a doctor—although no black woman had ever become one—and practice medicine in her hometown of Richmond. With this goal in mind, she worked towards, and received, a full scholarship to the New England Woman's Medical College in 1859.

With the outbreak of civil war in 1861, Lee left Boston to rejoin her family in Virginia, beginning a two-year interruption in her medical education. Upon returning to the college in 1863, she was shocked and dismayed to learn that the Board of Directors had revoked her scholarship.

Deprived of her only source of financial assistance, Rebecca was faced with the possibility of giving up her dream. However, she was able to continue her education after receiving a Wade Foundation grant after Benjamin Wade, a wealthy Ohio abolitionist, became interested in her case.

Another barrier to the completion of Lee's medical education was the obstacle of racial prejudice. Records of the New England Woman's Medical College dating from 1864 indicate that some faculty members were reluctant to grant Lee her medical degree.

Nonetheless, Lee's perseverance and dedication to her dream helped her to overcome these obstacles. On March 2, 1864, she received her medical degree, becoming the first American black woman in history to become a doctor.

After graduation, Dr. Lee left Boston and returned once again to Virginia, where she developed a thriving practice in her home city of Richmond. In doing so, she fulfilled a lifelong dream that few of her friends and family members thought could ever be realized. Dr. Lee had to overcome overwhelming odds to realize her goal of becoming a doctor and serving the needs of her people. Her perseverance and dedication in pursuing her goal serve as an inspiration to young blacks today as a testimonial to minority achievement.

Charles C. Spaulding (1874–1952), businessman, president of first black-owned multimillion dollar corporation

Born in Whitesville, Columbus County, N.C. on August 1, 1874—the third of fourteen children—Charles Clinton Spaulding knew the rigors of life on a farm. In winter, in addition to regular chores, he attended the local school session for black children.

Not content to remain on the farm, Charles went to the small village of Durham where, as a dishwasher in a hotel, he earned $10 a month. By saving his money, working afternoons and nights, he was able to attend school and graduated from the public schools of Durham in 1898.

After graduation, he became manager of a grocery company. The original supporters of the venture lost interest and eventually young Spaulding took over the company. His diligence and competence were recognized by others, which led him on to more important tasks.

When John Merrick, a barber, and Dr. A. M. Moore, a physician, decided to establish an insurance company for the benefit of, and owned, managed and operated by blacks, Spaulding became third member of the enterprise. This threesome started the North Carolina Mutual Life Insurance Company which was to become the first multimillion dollar corporation completely owned by blacks. In the beginning, Spaulding served in every capacity from janitor to office boy to salesman.

As the company grew, Spaulding served as General Manager. In August 1919, when John Merrick died, Spaulding was elevated to the position of secretary-treasurer. In 1923, upon the death of Dr. A. M. Moore, Spaulding advanced to president of the firm.

In 1931, Spaulding fulfilled a lifelong dream and visited Europe, thus broadening his already wide horizons. Absorbing the culture of the continent was not his only aim. Ever the business man, he also observed first-hand European business techniques.

In his lifetime, he received many awards as well as honorary degrees from Shaw University, Tuskegee Institute and Atlanta University. In addition, as a prominent executive he served in many community and philanthropic capacities. Explaining his climb from a poor farm to national prominence, Mr. Spaulding said, "Success is carved out with the chisel of efficiency, integrity and hard work." Death came in 1952 to this successful man.

Roland Hayes (1887–1977), classical tenor and pioneer in introducing Negro spirituals as concert music

Roland Hayes was born in Curryville, Georgia on June 3, 1887. His widowed mother, an ex-slave, eked out a meager living on a small farm to support her three children. Hunger and privation were no strangers to Roland, who had to begin working at the age of 9.

One day, while scrubbing floors in a white man's home, he heard an operatic selection on the phonograph. He was so thrilled by this glorious music, he decided then and there that he would become a professional singer of the classics.

Roland moved with his family to Chattanooga, Tennessee. Then 14, he paid 50¢ a lesson out of his meager earnings to study voice. He was eventually admitted to Fisk University and later toured with the Fisk Jubilee Singers.

In his desire to become an individual concert artist, Hayes rented Boston's Symphony Hall for $400 and performed his repertoire of spirituals, classical and romantic music to a packed house. But at this time singers weren't totally accepted without Europe's approval.

Using his entire savings of $1,100, Hayes sailed for England in 1920. After countless disappointments and with only one shilling left, he was summoned by King George V to give a command recital at Buckingham Palace. At last, he was recognized as a serious artist.

His first appearance after he returned to the U.S. was at New York's Town Hall. It was a sell-out and hundreds were turned away.

Hayes continued to captivate audiences with his sensitive interpretation of classical works, folk songs and Negro spirituals. He toured with the finest symphony orchestras in Europe and America. Said the Boston *Globe*, "Roland Hayes is not only an artist, he is an institution and a name, the magic of which has spread his fame across nations and continents."

Hayes was deeply concerned with the advancement of his people and hoped that his success would prove that blacks were capable of great accomplishments. His daughter, noted soprano Afrika Lambe, believes he paved the way for others—the noted Paul Robeson, for one.

Jesse Owens (1913–1980), athlete, Olympic gold medal winner

J. C. Owens was born into a family of Alabama sharecroppers. He was one of seven children and the grandson of slaves. J.C., as he was called, began working in the cotton fields at six and learned to read and write in a one-room schoolhouse between picking seasons.

When he was nine, his family moved to Cleveland, Ohio, where his father worked in a steel mill. Here his new grammar school teacher asked his name. "J.C.," he said in his Alabama drawl, which to her sounded like Jesse. And from that day on, Jesse is what he was called.

Jesse began running because, "We couldn't afford any kind of equipment, so we ran and ran." He entered his first formal competition at 13 and soon was setting records at East Technical High School. He won a scholarship to Ohio State and worked nights as an elevator operator to help pay his way. Here, under Coach Larry Snyder, Jesse soon earned the nickname, "The Buckeye Bullet."

In the spring of 1933, Jesse fell down a flight of stairs and injured his spine. It was the week before the Big Ten track and field meet at Ann Arbor, Michigan. His back was so sore he was afraid he couldn't bend over for the start of the race. Yet, despite the pain, he gave the greatest performance in a single day in the history of track athletics. He set three world records and tied one he had previously set. From that moment on, his goal was to run and jump in the Berlin Olympics.

Jesse was 22 when, before 120,000 spectators, he won four gold medals in the 1936 Olympic games. Some of the records he set would remain unbeaten for decades and they clearly upset Adolf Hitler's theory of white, Aryan racial superiority.

Returning home, Jesse found few jobs open to him. So he raced against horses and toured with the Harlem Globetrotters, giving half-time exhibitions. Eventually he founded his own successful public relations firm and acted as the State Department's "Ambassador to Sports."

President Ford presented the "Presidential Medal of Freedom" to him in 1976. And in 1979, he received the "Living Legends Award" from President Carter, who said, ". . . No athlete better symbolizes the human struggle against tyranny, poverty and racial bigotry."

11. Remember again the goals people in your family set and then, at the end of the last chapter, *planned* to achieve. Take out the paper on which you wrote *your* goal and *your* plans. Look them over to see if any re-planning is needed.

Now proceed to strive to achieve your goal, according to your plans. If you have already achieved it, great! Discuss how your plans and striving worked out and what you learned about achievement.

Now, *set* another goal, write it down (be sure it has the four characteristics of a short-range goal given on page 72), *plan* to achieve it, and then *strive* toward your goal. Use whatever you have learned in this chapter to help you strive effectively. In the next chapter you will have a chance to *evaluate* (Achievement Step 6) your setting, planning, and striving toward this goal.

Answers to Tangled String Games: #1: 1st car, A; 2nd car, B; 3rd car, C. #2: 1st dog, C; 2nd dog, A; 3rd dog, B. Game A: Man, A; Boy, D; Girl, B; Woman, C. Game B: Moose, A; Bear, D; Snake, B; Alligator, C. Game C: 1st bird, B; 2nd bird, D; 3rd bird, C; 4th bird, A.

8.

STEP 6.

EVALUATE

Achievers Evaluate Their Performance

Step 6 in achievement is to evaluate your performance. Achievers do this in order either to see how they can do a better job next time or to understand and feel that they did a good job and achieved their goal this time. They thereby strengthen their achievement motivation. Furthermore, evaluating their performance helps increase their sense of the future, their sense of where, as achievers, they may be heading.

Achievers may not do all this evaluating consciously. It's part of a developed attitude of mind: setting goals, planning, striving, and evaluating so as to achieve further and better.

Later, I shall be discussing ways to encourage children to take constructive, realistic looks at their efforts almost as a matter of habit—a habit of achievement.

■ *Achievement Conversations*

A good start for achievement-promoting conversation is to have members of the family say what specific things they, or other members of the family, do well. How do they know they do them well? Are there ways they could do them better? This is low-key evaluation.

121

You can ask your children questions about their accomplishments or goals achieved at almost any age. You might ask a four- or five-year-old, out of interest, *not* as an exam: "What things did you get done today?" or "this week," "since we came back," etc. Some answers might be: built a new truck out of blocks; beat Mary in a race; found ten good animal pictures in old magazines to use for a story; drew people pictures for the baby's room; said the alphabet all the way at kindergarten with only four mistakes and learned to correct mistakes; etc. Praise for these jobs well done, and interested questions about them, will help increase achievement motivation.

Then you can ask, probably first giving an example or two from your own activities, "Did you make any mistakes?" "Are there any things you might have done better?" Some answers might be: didn't note down my homework carefully so I did the wrong lesson; let the dirt dry on the dishes so it took me twice as long to wash them; watched a dumb TV program and so never got anything done on my sewing project; didn't telephone Aunt Sherilla in advance and so went all the way over to her house for some advice on baby-sitting and she was out; let two guys come over and play cards when I really wanted to work on my science project; put the baby to bed so fast she screamed and it took me twice as long to get her settled; etc. Again, praise for children's recognition of what they could have done better, and talking about it, with suggestions for even better ideas if they're asked for, or sometimes when they're not, helps reinforce a person's ability and desire to achieve.

Such conversations are usually (not always) best as a part of the ongoing activities of family life, not as staged events when they can become somewhat dull and stilted. If you keep achievement evaluation in your mind as a part of your agenda for bringing up children, opportunities will arise—around the table, while doing the dishes, in those relaxing moments at bedtime, on walks together, driving in the car. There's lots of room for good-natured laughter here. Even though the questions are basically serious, they can be asked lightly.

With very small children, as you watch them play, as they come to you to show you things, to ask for help, to complain, to laugh, or to be given a hug, you may find lots of opportunities to praise them for what are good achievements, let them explain or show how they reached their goals, or to ask them how they could have done a better job, or to make suggestions ("Suppose you put the big blocks on the bottom?" "Would standing on that little bench make it easier to clean the fish better?" etc.). Also, a very good question to ask, often, is "What are you going to do next?"

■ Was the Achievement a Responsible One?

A concept that children need to understand if their achievement motivation is to lead to good results is that of *responsibility*. They need to learn to ask: Was my goal a responsible one? Did I use responsible methods to achieve it? A responsible goal is one that is good for, not harmful to, oneself and others. Responsible methods are those that are good, not harmful, for self and others, both in the present and in the future.

For example, these *goals* would not be responsible because they would have had effects on others and/or oneself: to get a double helping of ice cream no matter how limited the supply; to get to talk for half an hour every night by phone to your boy- or girlfriend, no matter who needs the phone; to watch "Snortin' Mad" on TV every night no matter what anyone else wants to watch; to be in a swimming race even though you have an infected ear.

Examples of *methods* that would not be responsible because of bad effects would be: getting money to buy something by stealing it; pushing your way to the head of a line in order not to miss an important event; playing your radio while doing homework, thus keeping out other noises but disturbing others; borrowing your brother's or sister's equipment without permission; interrupting other people too much in order to win an argument; giving false information to others so that you can win something for yourself; copying somebody else's homework; cheating on tests.

123

■ *Developing a Sense of Responsibility*

Discussing with your children their own goals and actions, and those of other people whom you know, read about, or see on TV, including yourself, is an excellent way to develop the attitude of responsible achievement.

How can your children learn to know what the effects of their goals and methods will be on others? It's not always easy, and a good habit of evaluation is to keep asking, "What will this do to other people?" "Is this considerate of other people?" To be considerate of the needs and feelings of others, we and our children need to learn to put ourselves in the place of others, to imagine what it's like to be in their situation.

A favorite story of mine, which illustrates one child's rather limited sense of consideration of the needs of others, concerns seven-year-old Anya and her four-year-old brother Josh. The two children were in a large, busy, overheated department store, and they were holding melting double-dip ice-cream cones. Going down a crowded escalator, Anya crowded behind Josh, and Josh crowded behind a woman wearing an expensive mink stole. Anya looked at Josh and his dripping cone and whispered, "Watch out, Josh, you're getting fur all over your ice cream."

Well, Anya had learned to be moderately considerate of her brother. But she'd a way to go before she could put herself in the place of the mink-wearing lady.

A good way for children to develop the understanding needed to be truly considerate, and therefore responsible, is to role-play: to practice putting yourself in the situations of other people. You can ask questions like: "How do you think Mrs. Bergen felt when you did that?" "When Tara was late getting home because she wanted to finish her job, what do you think her father wanted to do?"

"Putting It into Practice" number 11 gives some role-playing exercises to help develop consideration and responsibility.

■ *Questions Achievers Ask Themselves as They
Evaluate*

It is useful to have in mind, or available to refer to, a list of
the questions achievers often ask themselves. These are questions
your children can learn to ask themselves, not necessarily all at
once, but as the way opens and habits of achievement develop.
They are questions you and your children can discuss together.
The discussion can be piecemeal and casual or, with older children from time to time, if they are interested, it can be fairly systematic, especially if the goal they strived for is a major and definite one.

Achievers' Questions

Did I achieve my goal?

What is the evidence that I did?

How well did I do on each step?

    1. Study yourself.

    2. Get goal ideas.

    3. Set a goal.

    4. Plan to achieve the goal.

    5. Strive to reach the goal.

    6. Evaluate your performance.

What did I do especially well?

How could I do better next time?

Was my goal a responsible one?

What were its effects on me? on others?

Were the methods I used responsible?

What new goals does my achievement lead to?

If I did not achieve my goal, why?

Could I have succeeded, or was it a case of unavoidable failure?

What can I learn from my failure to achieve it?

One point must be re-emphasized here. The objective in raising achieving children is to let them grow to be *independent* achievers. The motive to achieve must develop in them; it cannot be in-

jected into them by you. If you force them, they are likely to rebel. Be careful not to make a grim self-examination out of these evaluation questions, with you as examiner. Achievers examine themselves.

■ *Putting It into Practice*

1. As an exercise to be done by family discussion, or discussion between two or three members of the family, evaluate how well members act according to the *characteristics of achievers* that were explained in Chapter 2, "What Is Achievement Motivation? It's Learned, Not Inborn." Especially consider whether, since reading and discussing this book up to this point, there have been changes. Perhaps each person will want to jot down his or her other ratings on a separate sheet of paper.

CHARACTERISTIC	was strong already before reading book; needed no improvement	have improved	have not improved	don't think this characteristic is important for me
1. self-reliant and self-confident				
2. realistic about my strengths and weaknesses				
3. feel responsible for my own actions; don't blame or make excuses				
4. set challenging but possible goals				
5. plan carefully and intelligently				
6. take personal and world obstacles into account				
7. know how to find and use help				
8. keep striving, working toward goal				
9. check progress, not a wishful thinker				
10. enjoy achieving, dislike not achieving				
11. want to do a better and better job				
12. used achieved goals as basis for new goals to set and achieve				

As you discuss the various ratings, try to think of specific examples or incidents to illustrate them.

2. If you have a baby or very young child in the family or know one well enough to observe, evaluate the behavior of the child and compare it with the characteristics of achievers. Obviously, some of the characteristics are less applicable to little children than to older children and adults, but even babies show tendencies, sometimes quite spectacularly. The behavior of babies and little children is very interesting to talk about together in the family. Such talk, especially when based on actual events, helps indirectly to increase the achievement motivation and skills of those who are in the discussion.

3. Think back over the goal or goals that family members have actually set, planned for, work for, and achieved or failed to achieve, as a part of the activities in this book. In discussion, or in writing if anybody wishes, consider the goal in the light of the six achievement steps:

1. Study self; 2. Get goal ideas; 3. Set a goal; 4. Plan to achieve the goal; 5. Strive to reach the goal; 6. Evaluate your performance (what you are engaged in right now!).

As you think and discuss, try to remember specifically the two or three things you thought or did that were most useful, and then the two or three that were least useful or even harmful or wasteful. How would you avoid these harmful or wasteful things in the future? How might you use the ones that worked well?

4. Some time, when you are talking together, bring up the subject of unavoidable failures to achieve what seemed like realistic, medium-risk goals. Share experiences and what you learned from them that might strengthen your ability to achieve even though the failure was—yes—unavoidable. If you felt discouraged, how did you deal with that feeling? Did you get any positive feedback (from others, from your own remembering of past achievements and real strengths) that helped strengthen you as an achiever?

5. Somebody once said, "We fail toward success." What

might that mean? How can you learn from your mistakes? Share specific experiences of mistakes that taught you something.

6. Think back over your own experience and things you have seen, and choose one or two very specific examples of a job, perhaps a very simple one, done very well. Share these examples with your family.

It can be encouraging and amusing to choose examples from things you've seen members of your own family doing well. If there are those in the family who like to draw, perhaps posters could be made for each family member, titled "Peggy's Achievements" or "Jobs Kevin Does Well," or a better title, if you can think of one.

7. An exercise similar to #5 can be based on things that were done poorly. Remember, we learn from our mistakes. Think of a mistake of your own, tell about it, and tell what you learned from it, or should have learned. Artists: Do a poster on "Ways Our Family Has Learned from Mistakes."

8. On page 123, you read some examples of *irresponsible achievements,* either because of irresponsible goals or irresponsible methods used to achieve them. In a family discussion or as an achievement project, think of or try to find (from what you've observed at home, at school, or elsewhere, or from TV, newspapers, and magazines) examples of goals or methods that were harmful either to the achiever or to others, or to both. Tell what the goal was, what the method was, and why it was harmful.

In your discussion, try to think of ways that the goals or methods could have been made into responsible ones.

9. One can learn a lot from observing the behavior of children aged six to twenty-four months. If you can find the opportunity, watch a small child and note down any irresponsible goals it sets and actions it performs. Jot down or remember the details and tell what the harm was (or might have been if an older person hadn't helped the child get onto a more responsible track), and share these in conversation with others. Of course, everyone knows that babies aren't old enough to be very "responsible"; they can't think very well about future effects or effects on others.

As you discuss what you saw the little children doing, think what a responsible adult would have done in the same situation. Also discuss the question: How do little children learn to foresee the consequences of what they do?

10. Here are two more games from Sparling and Lewis's *Learningames*. They provide concrete ways to help develop in little children a sense of responsibility, an ability to foresee consequences and to think about the feelings of others.

Three to Four Years
A. MOVING AND SAYING

You may have used a fun path to give you an opportunity to tell the child words for positions in space. Now it's time for him to say the words. Use a *garden hose* or a *rope* to mark an interesting path, and as he follows it describe his moves: *through* the box tunnel, *under* the bench, *over* the block. Have him say the words first with you and later by himself. Then entice the child to new skills by adding new challenges to the fun path. Add a small plastic lid for standing on one foot, an inch-wide tape for walking-the-line, and parallel lines to begin and end a twenty-four-inch broad jump. Reposition the things occasionally to provide for new actions and to help him learn new positions. Now use more subtle position words as he walks: walk next to the box, jump away from the paper, in the middle of the loop, around the puddle, along the line. Walk him through it the first time you use the new position words. Then tell him as he goes again. When he's familiar with the actions, encourage him to say the words.

The child likes to invent new actions for himself, so when the path is rearranged he may have some suggestions of his own. He likes challenge, but if he doesn't feel sure of a new action he may avoid it for a while. To learn the words best he will need to hear and say them just at the moment he's engaged in doing them. If several children are playing, he might get confused unless the adult names actions for just one player at a time.

Goal: To increase the child's understanding of positions in space. To provide a pleasant and safe situation for physical development.

Uses: Ongoing physical development is essential to healthy growth of the child. Knowing the words for space relationships increases his understanding of situations and of instructions. "Go around the puddle to the car" is quite different from "Go to the car."

B. SEEING FEELINGS

For some time now you've probably been talking to the child about his feelings and about your own. The next step is to talk about the feelings of other children. The parent can point out the feelings of neighborhood children, and the teacher can point out feelings of classmates in the daycare center. When another child near your child displays a strong emotional expression, draw it to your child's attention. Lean down and say something like, "I think Matt looks very happy now, don't you?" That may be all of the conversation, or the two of you may talk for a moment about what made Matt so happy. Continue from time to time to point out feelings and to name them. If your child independently notices someone else's feelings, he deserves a compliment, such as, "You're paying good attention to other people. You know a lot about how they feel." It's especially helpful for the adult to comment on feelings that can be frightening to everyone. With your arm reassuringly around your child, explain, "Chris is so angry right now. That's called a tantrum. I think he will be over it soon." Sadness is not likely to be so threatening, but it can be puzzling. You might try saying, "Harry looks kind of sad—with tears in his eyes. I wonder if that's because he dropped his cupcake. I think I'll see if he needs some help. Would you like to come with me?"

Children "see" people around them expressing feelings. But they will need a lot of experience to accurately interpret them. Most children will not begin to use the names for others' emotions (happy, angry, sad) until the adult has used them for many months. Other names (joyous, suspicious, etc.) will take much longer. And just as with adults, the child will sometimes interpret incorrectly, but he's becoming aware.

Goal: To point out and name emotions when they occur in the child's peers. To help the child feel comfortable with frightening emotions in others.

Uses: The better we can "read" the emotional state of the people around us, the more successfully we can interact. Recogniz-

130

ing another's emotion is one step in the difficult task of taking another's point of view.

11. On page 124, you read about the usefulness of role-
playing as a method to understand the feelings and needs of other
people. If you are to be a responsible achiever, you need to learn
what the effects of your goals and methods are likely to be on
others, and this means trying to put yourself in their situation—"in their shoes," as the expression goes.

The next time there is an argument about something between two people in your family (or two friends), stop the argument (not so easy but worth a try!) and reverse roles. Then carry
on the argument, but argue from the point of view of the other
person as convincingly as you can. You must really try to see and
feel and think about it from the other's point of view.

Example of arguments might be: *Father vs. child:* whether the
child shall be allowed to have supper until she has picked up her
toys and done her chore of feeding the cat. *Brother vs. sister:*
whether sister can borrow brother's bicycle to ride over to a
friend's house to get help on homework when brother wants to
ride around on it after supper. Sister's bike is at the repair shop.
Mother vs. father: whether father should wash the dishes and see
that the kids get to bed (after he's been out working all day) so that
mother (who's been working at home all day) can get out of house
and play bridge with some friends.

After you do your role-plays, discuss what you learned from
them about responsible achievement.

12. Read the following story. It may be hard to believe, but
it really happened. After reading, discuss these questions about
the story: What was the goal of Navy men from Annapolis? Was it
a responsible one?

What means did the Navy men use? Were they responsible
ones? Be sure to explain your answer.

The Ghost of West Point

Every year there is a big football game between the teams of the Army officer-training school at West Point and the Navy officer-training school at Annapolis. It is called the Army-Navy game, and people in both schools make a big fuss about it.

One night in November of 1972, just a few days before the Army-Navy game, two young men were asleep in room 4714 at West Point. Suddenly they were wakened by a strange, hissing noise. They looked up and saw a ghost coming through the wall of the room! The ghost looked like a soldier from long ago, with an old-fashioned uniform and a big mustache.

The ghost stayed in the room for a few minutes and then disappeared. After it had gone, the air in the room felt cold. The two men went to the wall the ghost had come through, and the wall felt cold, much colder than the other three walls of the room. They knew that something very strange had happened, and they went to tell their friends.

At first no one believed the two men. The next day some other men agreed to spend the night in room 4714. Sure enough, there was a hissing noise, and the ghost appeared through the wall, and the wall was cold after it left. No one could explain how it had happened. Even people who said they didn't believe in ghosts thought that something supernatural was going on.

The men who ran West Point closed the room and didn't let anyone go into it. Everyone at West Point talked about the ghost, and there were big articles in newspapers all over the country. Everyone tried to figure out what was going on. Some men at West Point thought it was the ghost of a soldier who had gone to West Point a long time ago; they thought he had come back to visit the school.

Then, just before the Army-Navy game, the truth came out. The whole thing had been a trick by some men from Annapolis, the Navy training school. They were trying to "psyche out" the Army men so their team would lose the big game. The Navy men had lowered a slide projector outside the window of room 4714 and showed a slide of an old soldier through the window. They made the hissing sound and cold by using a fire extinguisher in an air shaft in the wall. The Army men felt pretty silly—but they still won the game.

13. Susan B. Anthony (1820-1906) was a major achiever in the field of human rights, especially for the rights of women to vote. In 1872, she was arrested for voting, since women at that time were not allowed to vote, despite the "voting rights amendment," the 14th Amendment, of the U.S. Constitution. It was not until 1920 that the 19th Amendment was passed, stating: "The right of citizens of the United States shall not be denied or abridged by the United States or by any state on account of sex."

Read the following story of what happened in 1872 when Susan B. Anthony led a group of women to vote. After you read the story, discuss these questions:

What was Susan Anthony's goal? Was it a responsible one?

In the story, what means did Anthony use to strive toward her goal? Were they responsible means?

On that important day in 1872, she [Susan B. Anthony] and her faithful followers cast their first ballots for President. But though the men in the polling place were momentarily moved, their minds were not yet opened. In a few days, Susan was arrested and brought before a judge, accused of having illegally entered a voting booth.

"How do you plead?" asked the judge.

"Guilty!" cried Susan. "Guilty of trying to uproot the slavery in which you men have placed us women. Guilty of trying to make you see that we mothers are as important to this country as are the men. Guilty of trying to lift the standard of womanhood, so that men may look with pride upon their wives' awareness of public affairs."

And then, before the judge could recover from this onslaught, she added, "But, Your Honor, *not* guilty of acting against the Constitution of the United States, which says that no person is to be deprived of equal rights under the law. Equal rights!" she thundered. "How can it be said that we women have equal rights, when it is you and you alone who take upon yourselves the right to make the laws, the right to choose your representatives, the right to send only sons on to higher education. You, you blind men, have become slaveholders of your own mothers and wives."

The judge was taken aback. Never before had he heard these ideas expressed to him in such a forceful manner. However, the law was the law! The judge spoke quietly, and without much conviction. "I am forced to fine you one hundred dollars," he said.

"I will not pay it!" declared Susan Anthony. "Mark my words, the law will be changed!" And with that, she strode from the court.

"Shall I follow her and bring her back?" the court clerk asked the judge.

"No, let her go," answered the elderly judge. "I fear that she is right, and the law will soon be changed."

PART III

Achievement Motivation and Some World Realities

We have seen that achievers are self-reliant, self-starting, rather independent people. They prefer to set their own goals rather than have others set goals for them. They are not docile Pawns. A major challenge for them is to use their achievement energy and ambition in responsible ways. That means setting goals and using methods that are good, not harmful, for themselves and others, both now and in the future.

However, achievers must deal with those parts of the "real world" that do not value independence, that stress obedience. They must deal with goals imposed upon them by others, at home, at school, on the job, in the community, and with the rules and laws that home, school, jobs, and community need. Often these rules and laws are good and necessary. Part III deals with these challenges.

It deals, also, with a key question for young people of school age and their parents: how parents and teachers can work together or apart to encourage students to become and stay strong achievers.

Lastly, in the light of what has been explained in the book, we again address the questions: Is it ever too late to convert a non-achiever into an achiever? Is it ever too early to start? The answer to both questions is *no*. Because of that, we can start at any time to build the builders of a more productive, satisfying, challenging, and enjoyable world for the individual and for everyone.

9.

How Achievers Deal with Goals and Rules Imposed by Others

There's little question that both children and adults, but especially children, need some firm, consistent limits on their behavior to help govern their lives and provide them with physical and emotional stability and security. Achievers need to learn that their initiative usually must be expressed and their goals set and strived for within the boundaries of certain rules and laws. An obvious example is traffic laws. Another is respect for property. Yet another is the expectation that you will tell the truth. Without these governing expectations, life would be chaotic, and in general, more harm than good comes from chaos. But as I've already made clear, the opposite of chaos doesn't have to be Pawnlike obedience to the rules and requirements.

■ *Rules and Requirements at Home*

From the age that children begin to be able to control their own behavior, they will learn that daily living in the family works better for them and others if it is ordered by some definite expectations, both stated and unstated. Some of these, somewhat in order of priority, are:

(1) Stay out of dangerous places—for young children, for example, a traffic-filled street.

(2) Tell the truth.

(3) Respect other people's property; don't borrow without permission unless you're sure the owner won't mind.

(4) Respect people's privacy—and expect them to respect yours.

(5) Don't raid the refrigerator or eat family food without an understanding of what you may and may not have for between-meal snacks.

(6) Do your chores, and do them well.

(7) Abide by the laws of the community and the agreements in the family about drinking.

(8) Abide by family policies about smoking.

(9) Share your things (toys, equipment) if you can; it will help people have fun, get their jobs done, and reach their goals.

(10) Don't use language that is offensive to others.

(11) Don't interrupt people unless it's important or likely to be helpful.

(12) Don't monopolize the telephone.

(13) Clean up your own messes and put things away.

(14) Be on time for meals and other occasions, or explain in advance why you won't be.

(15) Play quietly if noise will bother others.

(16) Go to bed when you're supposed to unless there are important reasons not to.

(17) Keep reasonably clean; if you're dirty, get cleaned up.

The list could be lengthened—or, in some families, shortened. It will be different in different families, with different ages. "Putting It into Practice," number 3, gives the family a chance to evaluate these rules.

■ *How to Make and Deal with Rules and Requirements*
Clearly, no child will be perfect in sticking to and behaving according to all these rules and expectations. With increasing age and maturity—and sometimes with spectacular lapses during crises—creative respect for them will increase. Don't expect three-year-olds to self-govern their living by all of these; a ten-year-old will do much better; a fourteen-year-old, in a period of adolescent limits-testing and confusion, may do much worse for a while.

Parents can be most helpful by making clear what has to be clear (no running out into street traffic; no stealing); by discussing and explaining and teaching rather than merely commanding; by being sure to praise and give good feedback for good, constructive behavior rather than taking it for granted and merely scolding or punishing children for their lapses. When children fail to meet expectations, it's best to talk about it, to let the child describe what he or she did that was wrong, and then to agree on how to do better next time. Or perhaps it will turn out that the rule or expectation was wrong, unrealistic, or too limiting, and needs to be changed.

Also, it's almost always best, if possible, to work with your children of any age to set up the rules and expectations *in advance* of an emotional or behavioral crisis. For example, with a teenager, the time to work out sensible policies (about going out, getting home, letting your parents know where you are, hours and activities, and transportation) is when it is possible to have a calm, reasonable discussion of the whole situation, with plenty of give and take, and no immediate, specific issue to decide. It's a good idea to write down what you agree upon so that when there is a

141

crisis later, you and your children can refer to what you agreed to when you were considering the matter calmly and reasonably.

■ *Dealing with Minor Crises*

Of course, though, there will sometimes be crises, especially if you have encouraged children to show initiative, set their own goals, and plan and strive on their own. It's interesting to know that in Chinese our word *crisis* is expressed by two symbols, the one for *danger* and the one for *opportunity*. Families that raise achieving children will find ways to deal with the danger so that no one is seriously harmed, but to take advantage of the opportunity for growth in understanding and initiative for achievement.

Let's take an example. Eleven-year-old Jaime lets five of his friends come into the house to play on a rainy afternoon. They get hungry, so they eat most of the cake his mother had made for supper and also drink up all the milk in the refrigerator. Therefore, at supper time comes a minor crisis. An achievement-squelching response to the crisis would be an angry laying down the law and dictated punishment: no more friends in for a week, no dessert for Jaime for the next three suppers, and Jaime is sent to his room for an hour after supper. Furthermore, here's how you're going to deal with such situations in the future: and you, the parent, *tell* 'em! And then you threaten punishment if the dictated procedures aren't followed.

There's another way to deal with the crisis. It, too, might well involve anger: that's a part of reality, and taking it into account is a part of responsible achievement. But then could come the constructive part of using the crisis. You talk it over and work out a solution for next time:

> Why did you eat the cake and drink the milk?
> I needed to feed my hungry friends.
> Did you know the rules about eating between meals?
> Yes.
> Are they responsible rules?
> I suppose so; the family's got to eat and Mom has to plan.

O.K., good! So what was your goal?

To feed my friends.

What other ways could you have done it and still not ruined supper?

And Jaime figures: look on the snack shelf and use what was there. But since it wasn't enough, figure out how to get more. Maybe open a box of crackers and a can of fruit juice, if there's plenty. Offer to pay for them later out of my allowance. Maybe take up a collection and let a couple of the kids go to the corner store to buy some snacks.

Good! Great ideas! Is there anything Mom can do to help in such situations in the future?

Well, maybe we could have an emergency food supply. I'll put some money in from my savings to keep it up. Hey, maybe I could be in charge of the emergency food supply and everybody in the family could help pay for it.

Good idea!

You see the approach: You and your children deal with reality; you work through the anger; some goals are set; plans are made for how to achieve them; using help is considered; and so forth—with plenty of positive feedback for good ideas and initiative.

In general, the approach is *discussion, goal-setting,* and *planning.* What didn't work? What were your goals? How could you achieve them within the rules and requirements? Are the rules and requirements reasonable? If not, do they need changing? If they are reasonable, can you make them your own and use them as you achieve? What help might you use? What will the effects be on you and others?

In "Putting It into Practice," there are some other examples of goals and rules imposed by others with exercises to help children think through how to deal with them and still to strengthen achievement motivation.

143

■ *Dealing with Goals and Rules Imposed by Jobs and by the Community*

Perhaps to an even greater extent than in families, jobs and activities in the community impose goals and actions on people. How do achievers deal with these impositions—usually necessary, sometimes arbitrary and foolish, but nonetheless real? The basic technique they use is to try to make the goals and actions their own on responsible terms. First, of course, they must realize they are necessary. An example of necessary goals on a job might be to produce a required amount of work of a required standard of quality with a set period of time. You must cut the grass, rake the cuttings, weed the garden, and leave things neat and ready for next time, all between 9:30 and 12:30 on Saturday morning; those are the conditions. Another example of an imposed goal might be to pass a physical fitness test or information and aptitude test in order to be eligible for a job, say as a factory office worker. That job might, in turn, be a goal on the road to a longer-term goal in the world of business or professions. If the achievers really want to achieve their longer-term goal, they will make the short-term goal their own; they will accept it, set it as if for themselves, and plan and strive to achieve it. It becomes a part of their own longer-range plans and goals.

In general for jobs, imposed or required behavior will include being on time, doing what you say you will, working steadily and being productive. Otherwise, unless your relative owns the place or you have some sort of utter job security arrangement, you aren't likely to keep the job. And if you can demonstrate the characteristic of achievers of trying always to do a better and better job, you are more likely to be promoted and do well.

With imposed goals, achievers consciously or unconsciously tend to use these means to achieve them:

• They decide whether the goal is necessary and responsible.
• If it is, they make the goal their own.
• If the goal is too high-risk for them (nearly impossible to achieve), they try to get it modified so that it will be medium-risk: challenging but possible.

• They then plan and strive to achieve the goal.

• They get any help they may need to achieve the goal—help that will strengthen them, not weaken them. They don't try to get someone to do the job for them.

■ Teaching Young Children to Deal with Imposed Goals

From as early as children are able to talk fluently, they can be taught to plan and strive to achieve necessary goals. Basically, when a child protests, "I don't see why I hafta . . . ," your answer can be, "Well, there *is* a reason. See if you can figure it out. Why *do* you have to . . . ?" And when the child does figure it out, give plenty of praise and feedback. If the child can't figure it out, explain simply, and then ask the child to say the explanation in his or her own words and praise the accurate explanation.

Let's take an example. Six-year-old Gina has set her own goal: to be allowed to ride her tricycle up and down the sidewalk of the block in front of her house all by herself. You're worried that she may lose control and go into the street or that she may leave her cycle on the sidewalk where it may be damaged or taken. So you say that before she can do that, she must accomplish two things: be able to ride up and down the front walk without going off into the grass, and always put her bike beside the porch steps when she stops using it—and that she must achieve these goals steadily for a week. If Gina says, "Why do I hafta?" have her explain, and praise her explanation, if it's correct.

Other examples: Seven-year-old Matthew wants to be allowed to take off the shelves any books in the house that interest him and look at them. You make him first set an interim goal of keeping the books in his own room in order and in good condition, which he thinks is a bother.

Five-year-old Amelia wants two goldfish of her own. You require her first to learn to care well for the family goldfish on the kitchen windowsill and show you each day that she's done so.

Remember, at any age, the more figuring out of things for themselves you let your children do, the more strongly they will be motivated to achieve, provided they are not faced with tasks far beyond their ability. Remember, too, that despite the necessity to achieve goals set by others, the most important thing, if you want achieving children, is to give them independence, within safe limits, to explore, to set goals, and to achieve on their own, with you parents as encouragers, pleased with good goals well planned for, worked for, and achieved.

■ *Two Examples, One Bad, One Good*

It's useful sometimes to look at the adult world and see how people respond to goals they somehow feel society has imposed upon them, or that they have to achieve in order to make it in society. A tragic example of achievement motivation gone wrong is that of Dr. John Roland Darsee. At age thirty-three, he was considered one of the most promising heart specialists in the country. He'd published dozens of scientific papers. And then his medical colleagues gradually discovered that he had faked his data. He had claimed to have performed heart experiments on dogs that he'd never really done. He merely killed the dogs and made up the charts as if he had actually completed experiments. His charts and his proofs were "too good to be true," and he was caught. Darsee had succumbed to the pressure that he felt was imposed by the scientific and medical professions to produce published studies. When he was detected, he explained:

"I had too much to do, too little time to do it in, and was greatly fatigued mentally and almost childlike emotionally. I had not taken a vacation, sick day, or even a day off from work for six years. I had put myself on a track that I hoped would allow me to have a wonderful academic job and I knew I had to work very hard for it. Successful people don't take time off—at least that's the premise on which I based my work."

The lesson from this is that we parents must try to be sure that our children strive well to achieve challenging goals, yes, but that they do not go to extremes, that they are encouraged to relax, take time for pleasure and friendship and humor—and, now and then, just being lazy.

A good example of people being effectively encouraged to achieve goals imposed by the realities of business is found in a memo recently addressed by the president of a large corporation to his senior management group. He tells them that the goal (an imposed one) is "winning and retaining customers" with "good service at a fair price." And then he writes: "I expect each of you [managers] to support your people's success, to recognize and reward good performance while helping to improve performance." He says he wants his people to be "thoughtful risk-takers," but also "strongly results-oriented," and he sees the basic responsibility of managers as that of "creating a work environment that allows employees to use their talents to the fullest and thus encourage their motivation.

■ *Putting It Into Practice*

1. In a discussion with members of your family, think of two or three goals or rules that are imposed upon you and that you accept as necessary. Why were they imposed on you rather than your choosing them for yourself? At what age were they imposed? How have you made yourself able to accept them? Use experiences from anywhere except school, since we'll be discussing school in the next chapter.

2. Try to think of an achievement goal or a rule that is imposed on you that you do not really accept and "make your own," even though you may submit to it out of necessity. Why was it imposed on you? Why do you not accept it willingly? If you talk about it long enough with the person who imposed it, do you think you could either:

• get it changed? or
• be persuaded that it is necessary and good?

3. On pages 140–141 is a list of seventeen home-imposed rules and requirements. On a separate sheet of paper, write numbers 1 to 17 and beside each number indicate how you rate each item, thus:

SA = strongly agree
A = agree
D = disagree
SD = strongly disagree

Compare your ratings with those of others in the family and discuss them. Can you persuade any people to change their ratings? Can anyone persuade you? Would you add any rules or requirements with which you would strongly agree? If so, write them on your sheet and discuss them.

4. In your family, how do people actually treat goals or regulations that are imposed upon them and with which they disagree? How do you think they should treat them? Discuss this.

5. Has any imposed rule or requirement ever prevented you from achieving a responsible, important goal that you chose for yourself? Explain.

6. Has any member of your family ever broken an imposed rule or refused to achieve an imposed goal? What was it? What happened? If the family had it to do over again, would anyone behave differently? Discuss this with your family.

7. In your family, or any others that you know of, are there any requirements or goals that children eighteen and under impose on their parents? If so, discuss them and say what you think of them.

8. Think of an achievement that was imposed on a member of your family that was just impossible for that person to perform successfully, but where, after the person explained, the requirement was changed so that it became an achievable goal. Who suggested the change and what was it? After the change, was the person able to make the goal his or her own?

(*Examples:*

• Three-year-old Mimi simply was unable to make her bed neatly without spending so long that she got very angry. So the requirement was changed: Mimi only had to put away her pajamas, pull up the sheet and blankets, and put the pillow in place, but not tuck it all in and put on a bedspread. After these changes, she worked hard to keep her room in order.

• Ralph was required to practice for an hour and a half a day if he was to be allowed to take trumpet lessons. However, his school homework, household chores, and his desire for some time to be with his friends made this impossible. So Ralph proposed two hours a day on weekends and two half-hour periods on other days unless homework was extra hard, in which case he practiced just half an hour. His parents accepted this arrangement, and Ralph felt part of the decision and, according to his teacher, made excellent progress on the trumpet.)

9. Read again on pp. 144–145 the five ways that achievers use to make an imposed goal their own so that they are ready to plan and strive for it. Write or tell a story, true or fictitious, of someone who used these five ways. Or, make a poster, or five smaller posters, illustrating the five ways.

10. Think about requirements that are necessary and therefore imposed on a person in order to hold a job or to live or serve in your community. To find an example, talk with an adult who holds a job or serves the community and ask these questions: Is there anything you are required to do, or to achieve, in order to hold your present position? Do such requirements keep you from achieving important goals that you set for yourself? How have you adjusted to these requirements? Are there any you are working to get changed? Note down the answers and discuss them with your family.

11. Read this true news columnist's report on the career of an automobile dealer. After you've read it, discuss the questions that follow.

A Car Dealer's Unselfish Side
by Frank Rossi

A lot of mail comes in about people who sell cars. "Let me tell you about the crummy rat who sold me a car," is how most of these letters start out. The one about Dan Polett was different.

Dan Polett owns Wilkie Buick, which does business in a not-so-terrific neighborhood on North Broad Street.

"About five years ago," the letter started, "after a drunk

driver totaled my car, Dan loaned me a demo for over six months until I was able to buy another one. At that time, if it wasn't for the use of that demo both Peg and I would've been up the crick.

"Aside from the help he's given me, I've been impressed with the way he's treated the people in his company."

Wilkie Buick is like Fort Apache. It encloses almost a whole block, and there's only one way in and out. When Dan Polett bought the business in 1970, the neighborhood was grungy. It's less so now, but it's still no great shakes.

"Have you ever thought of moving out?"

"Yeah," Dan Polett says. "I've thought about that a lot. I wouldn't consider starting a business here today, because I don't think it would succeed. . . . But we're quite successful here, so it's hard to talk in terms of disadvantages when you're doing well—and we've done well for many years."

So while the others were running for the suburbs, Polett stayed and prospered.

Dan Polett grew up in North Jersey, didn't have much when he was a kid, cut lawns to help his mother with expenses. When he was 15, his mother died, leaving Dan and his two older brothers alone.

He lived with his brothers, worked his way through college and got a job with General Motors. It was as if the only thing he knew was work—16 hours a day he was at it. He climbed fast and was on his way to corporate superstardom when the chance to buy Wilkie Buick came up. He took it.

Wilkie had a good reputation but didn't sell many cars. Polett changed that. Today he sells more Buicks than any other dealer in his three-state region. Wilkie is among the top 50 Buick dealerships in the country.

Ask Dan Polett about his success. He talks about integrity, value, cordiality. But they're just words, and any fly-by-night can use them for free. Beyond that, however, Polett can't explain it.

The little stories they tell about Dan Polett explain it better.

First, to clear things up up front. Dan Polett works his ears off and he expects, and usually gets, as much from the people who work for him. He has fired people who can't cut it. On the other hand, Wilkie Buick has little employee turnover—the average worker has been there 11 years.

Story No. 1: Seven years ago, Frank Longbottom, one of Wilkie's best engine and transmission mechanics, came to Dan Polett. Longbottom was a top man earning good pay, but he wanted more. He wanted his own business. Dan Polett might have been hurt or angry. He might have told Longbottom to take a powder.

But Polett didn't want to lose Longbottom, so instead he offered him a deal. Longbottom could operate his transmission business out of Wilkie Buick. Today, Frank Longbottom works all day as a mechanic for Wilkie. At night he builds transmissions for himself.

Wilkie Buick buys many of those transmissions—and, says Polett, they're cheaper and better than the transmissions Wilkie was buying before Frank Longbottom started his own business.

Story No. 2: Actually, this is several stories. A car with a Wilkie Buick insignia is broken down. A Wilkie mechanic passes. The mechanic stops to help.

Story No. 3: Jay Dunphy worked for Polett 12 years. He was general manager, and he's gone as far as he could go. "I really want an opportunity to run something myself, but I don't have what I need to put it together. Would you encourage me to try? Would you discourage me?"

Polett knew what to do. He put up some money and went to the bank with Dunphy for the rest. Dunphy opened a Ford dealership in the Northeast. Dunphy Ford has been successful, which is good for Dunphy and Dan Polett.

The same thing happened with Garth Seidel, who had been Wilkie's general manager and vice president. A few months ago, with Polett's backing, he opened Center City Chevrolet.

That's what you call spreading the faith.

Now discuss these questions, or just think about them as they apply to yourself and achievement.

(a) The subject of this chapter is goals and rules imposed by others. What evidence is there in the story that Dan Polett had to accept goals and conditions he did not choose himself? (Hint:

151

What does the term "Fort Apache" mean?) Look for evidence not only in his automobile dealership but also in his earlier life.

(b) At what point in Polett's career did he choose to achieve on his own rather than take the chance to get rich in a large organization? (Hint: Look for the word "superstar.") Would you have made that choice?

(c) What evidence is there in the story that Polett *planned* (Achievement Step 4) and *strived* (Achievement Step 5)?

(d) What is Polett's long-range goal? Is he making it? Do you think the goal is responsible? Explain.

(e) How does Polett deal with people working in his dealership who want to strike out and set their own goals? Give examples.

(f) Which kind of competition do you think is most important to Polett: competition with others; competition with his own past performance; competition with a standard of excellence.

(g) What do you think Polett means by these three words: integrity; value; cordiality. How might each of them help him achieve his goals?

(h) The title of the story is "A Car Dealer's Unselfish Side." What does the word "unselfish" mean in Polett's case? Has his "unselfishness" helped him or hindered him in achieving his goals? Explain.

10.

Working with the School to Strengthen Achievement Motivation

This is a book for parents and their children, not primarily a book for teachers, although teachers certainly should consider it one of their main jobs to educate students to achieve. In fact, with this conviction in mind, in 1983 David McClelland and I wrote three school workbooks that provide teachers and students with a series of lessons designed to strengthen achievement motivation and skills. They are titled *Learning to Achieve*. One is for grades 4–7, one for 6–9, and one for 9–12. If your child's school is using these books, it would be useful for you to ask to see them so that you can

*Published by Scott, Foresman & Co., 1900 E. Lake Avenue, Glenview, IL 60025, © 1984.

153

help reinforce at home the achievement lessons that your children are doing at school.

■ How Achievement Competence Training (ACT) Worked in Schools

At the beginning of Part II, I mentioned the Achievement Competence Training (ACT) program developed by Research for Better Schools, and based on the work of McClelland and others. Where the program was used, it was successful, as were other Mc-Clelland-inspired programs carried out with inner-city and suburban groups in Boston and St. Louis. Why, then, did they not spread, since lack of student motivation is one of the main concerns of teachers and parents about school students? McClelland says: "The reasons for the failure of an effective educational program to spread are complex but derive in part from the fact that teachers are primarily interested in presenting subject matter, not in developing general adaptive traits in children."

However, the ACT program was field tested in some 104 classrooms in 42 public schools in all sorts of communities in five states, but mostly in the greater Philadelphia area. Here are some accounts of actual interviews with teachers:

[A pupil of mine, **Jeff**,] "recounted a story about how he had gone with his parents to visit some relatives. While the adults were talking, he went out with his cousin, who introduced him to some friends. These children had started to build a playhouse but got fed up with the job and left it half-finished. Jeff upbraided them and told them they needed to use a striving method. When asked what that was, he explained about the lessons called ACT he had at school. He then proceeded to tell them about planning and the other steps. Before leaving, he got them not only to set a goal to get the playhouse finished, but also to make a plan and actually get working on the thing again."

Debbie told me that she had been surprised and pleased with the results of the Strength Survey. She hadn't realized before how

155

many strengths she did have. She also said that learning about risk had made her realize that some of the work she did for a social studies project was really too easy. In one instance, she had redone a report to make it work of a higher standard.

Another teacher, *Russell Scaramastra,* reported an instance in which ACT training helped children to work together more effectively. One of his reading groups was to put on a play for the class. Some members of the group were in the ACT class, while others were not. At first the children bickered and argued about how the play should be put on. Finally, a boy who had been a group leader in the ACT class suggested that they choose a group leader to get things written down. The others agreed, and the group began to plan for the play. It was obvious, Mr. Scaramastra said, that the initiative was taken by children who were in the ACT program.

Scaramastra has also found that the project work of his class is of a much better quality. This change he also attributes to ACT because he had not directly talked about or practiced behaviors or strategies for improving project work. "ACT gives you a basis to spring from," he explained.

In general, parents reacted well to the ACT program. The mother of a boy in the ACT class claimed that her son was awake for the first time in years. She had noticed a sudden and startling change in his accomplishments in school. This change was mostly due, she felt, to maturational factors and the fact that he had overcome some learning problems he had as a young child. Nevertheless, she felt that ACT had helped also. It had given him a strategy that he could apply to his life both in school and at home.

The boy's counselor, as well as his teacher, also recognized the change. The counselor now works to help the youngster set goals in academic areas and to help him achieve them. The boy himself is very positive about the program. He felt that much of his success was due to his having taken ACT.

And here is a letter, according to an ACT report, "typical of the general feeling of support expressed by many parents."

We are thrilled with all you are doing. The new program being used on fifth graders has been 100 percent successful. We can see Tom feeling purposeful, proud of himself, and wanting to accomplish what is expected of him. The beauty of all this—there doesn't seem to be any pressure.

And here, to end this informal survey of actual experiences in achievement training, are comments by a teacher and by a student:

Teacher
Students who lacked self-confidence were helped most. Setting goals was a constant reminder. It had to come from within them. There was carry-over in other areas. Setting goals has become part of everyday routine.
Student
For almost three years my dad said he was gonna take us ice fishing but he never did it, so I got one of those achievement worksheets and filled it out and we did it.

A teacher in Berea, Ohio (a heterogeneous suburb of Cleveland), whose class I visited and who was using the ACT materials, said, "There's a desperate need for materials like this. The kids have no idea how to set goals and to work for them." But when I asked why the school didn't just adopt the materials, she said, "Because we're curriculumed up to here," holding her hand at the bridge of her nose.

Perhaps that's enough to suggest how some teachers and parents felt about the achievement training program, and they certainly make it sound desirable. Of course, parents don't run schools (and it's certainly just as well). But there are ways in which you can encourage and teach your children to use their experiences and lessons at school to strengthen their motivation to achieve, and there may be ways, too, in which you can help teachers who want your children to become achievers.

157

■ *The Impact of Entering School*

There's no doubt that many schools are achievement squelchers. Sometimes it is because of conditions in the community that seem to give them no other choice than to impose rigid orders. Sometimes it is because they seem to value simple obedience above all, a set program, answers fixed in the textbook or in the teacher's mind, and because they discourage initiative and responsibility on the part of students unless it be entirely on the teachers' terms. This sort of school is epitomized by the story of a teacher who asked his third-grade class, "What numbers between one and ten can be divided by two?" An eager student raised her hand. "Yes, Andrea," said the teacher. "Seven," said Andrea. "Seven!" exclaimed the teacher, with scorn in his voice. "How can seven be divided by two?" "Seven divided by two is three-and-one-half," said Andrea, to which the teacher's response was, "All right, Andrea, if you're going to be smart, you can leave the room."

Unhappily, there are many people in some communities, especially among the powerless and the poor, who feel a need to have the schools provide rigid discipline, demand obedience, and even discourage creative thinking. Ways must be found to show people that simple order and obedience do not encourage achievement but tend to squelch it. Kim Marshall, in his book *Law and Order in Grade 6-E* (Boston: Little, Brown, 1972) compares such schools to "tidal pools near the ocean, in which a marvelous and colorful variety of marine life flourishes—crabs, underwater flowers, and so forth—when the water is calm. . . . The effect of a strict disciplinarian on kids [is] . . . similar to the effect of the incoming tides on these pools: the flowers close up tight, the crabs run into cracks and caves, and everything becomes still and colorless."

Fortunately, however, there are a great many schools where students are encouraged to be smart, to show initiative, to set challenging goals on their own, and to plan and strive within the requirements of the curriculum and the limits of manageability—schools where life is *not* still and colorless.

158

However, as I said earlier, studies show that most children enter kindergarten or first grade feeling rather good and optimistic about themselves, but by the time they reach third or fourth grade, or maybe seventh or eighth, they've been made either docile or rebellious. Too often, in the name of imposed order and standards, they've been made into Pawns instead of Origins.

Some of the situations to which children will probably and quite properly need to adjust when they enter school are:

a powerful adult, backed by a definite system, to whose demands they must conform;

a large group of people of their own age with whom they compete and compare themselves, and with whom the system compares them;

a teacher who is evaluating their performance and behavior objectively, according to standards and not on a personal, family basis, as a parent does;

or, on the contrary, a situation where there are many more chances to be free and make mistakes and get into trouble (or be gotten into trouble by others) than there ever were at home.

Unfortunately, there are also schools that present a completely undemanding situation where all you have to do to get along is be quiet, be obedient, and perform your routine tasks—tasks the point of which you may not understand and not have a chance to discuss.

■ *Helping Children Use School to Strengthen Achievement Motivation*

Of course, there are many children who have been raised so well, with love and toughness, with challenges and opportunities to set and achieve goals, with positive, realistic feedback for jobs they do well, and with the sort of help that strengthens them, that they are ready to get the most out of school, whether it be too rigid, too loose, or just right. Especially with such children, but

159

with all others also, parents must be careful not to be too interfering in their children's school. Children have to learn how to cope with school; the parents' contribution is to help their children strengthen themselves so that they can cope.

Here are some initial suggestions for what parents can do.

Stay informed. Read everything that the school sends home, by mail or by child. Arrange to visit the school, but probably not your own child's class. Ask for a statement of the school's goals and curriculum and for any other materials that the school has that describe it. Attend parents' meetings. Engage your children in conversation about what goes on at school—not "What did you learn today?" but more like, "So how was school today? Anything you specially liked? Any problems?"

The purpose of your staying informed is to have the background you need to encourage your children to take advantage of what the school offers, and to strengthen them in dealing with the problems they face.

Express your expectations. Keep in mind that a great many teachers and principals feel that one of their greatest problems is the lack of concern in many students' home environment. These produce children who don't seem to care, who don't read, don't do homework, watch too much TV, and just hack off. If yours is not such a family, let it be known. Let it be known that you have high expectations for your children, based on facts, and that you hope the school will, too. Children tend to achieve according to what is expected of them. Be open, though, to the possibility that your expectations may seem to the school to be too high or too low. If this is a problem, get the facts from the school, give the facts you know, and talk about it with your children.

Confer with people at school. To stay informed and to exchange expectations, conferences are useful. If you are invited to confer with teachers or someone else at school, make every effort to go. **Listen** and absorb what you are told. **Answer** questions as factually as you can. **Ask** whether the school thinks your child is achieving up to his or her ability. **Ask** whether any action is required of you or, more importantly, of your child. **Follow up** the

conference with a note to the school thanking them for the conference and stating briefly whatever actions, if any, you understand
you will be taking, your child will be taking, and the school will be
taking. Be sure that your child is told specifically what was agreed
on and has a chance to discuss it with you. This is a part of the reality of the child's life.

I think that usually, if the child is eight or nine years old or
older and if there is not some deeply troubling matter to confer
about (for example, whether psychiatric help should be sought),
children should be present at the conferences of their parents and
teachers. If they are present, they can hear the information, the
concerns, the good and bad news, they can answer for themselves
if they wish to, and they will be informed at once. If they are not
present, they'll get two versions, one from the teacher and one
from the parent, or they may never get any version at all. Generally, I think we underestimate the ability of children to absorb and
deal with information and opinions about themselves, and to express convictions about themselves.

■ School Requirements

In Chapter 9, I discussed how achievers can cope with goals
and rules imposed by others. Most school situations impose many
requirements. They have to, if large numbers of people are to
work together effectively. Some of them are quite obvious, and
quite like those for living in the home or in the community: be on
time; be where you're supposed to be; follow directions; ask if you
don't understand; do your classwork and your homework; raise
your hand if you want to say something; respect the property of
others, of yourself, and of the school; pass the work in all subjects
if you can. Further, there are rules having to do with such matters
as dress, eating, gum, radios, running, bad language, alcohol and
drugs, fighting, cheating, and leaving the campus or the classroom. Most, though not all, achieving people will try to go by the
rules and obey them, since they know that getting the most out of
school and graduating with a good record is a goal they can set for

161

themselves as an important step toward long-range goals more independently set.

However, if achievers see some rules and requirements as blocking their goals and ambitions, or as making out-of-school goals more difficult to plan and strive for, most of them will work to get the achievement-squelching rule or requirement changed. But until it is changed, they abide by it.

It may help children to strengthen their achievement motivation if they have opportunities to talk over with you whatever they see as preventing them from setting and achieving their own goals. For example, your daughter may be very much involved in getting to the climax of a science project and want to invest a lot of time in the exciting work of planning and striving for her goal. But she may find that routine drill and homework on some aspect of math or English that she has already mastered is, she feels, wasting her time. Or your son may have ambitions as a trumpet or piano player and need a lot of time to practice, but find that routine school work is getting in the way. Other goals (a community gardening project, a research trip for history, etc.) may be interfered with by what your child sees as time-wasting school activities. Talking these over with you may enable children or students to plan a solution. You may suggest ideas, but in most cases the solution should be worked out by the young developing achiever. Also, it may be the occasion for a parent-student-teacher conference. "Putting It into Practice" at the end of the chapter gives some specific situations to work through.

■ *Homework or No Homework*

Some searchers for solutions to the weaknesses of schools simply assert that there should be "more homework," yet nothing can be more deadening to achievement motivation than quantities of routine, mindless homework—imposed busyness. The legitimate purposes of homework—which could better be called "independent work," for it can be done anywhere, even in the classroom—are: to provide time for reading and doing "study" material such as in history, science, English, or math; to practice and master skills or content taught at school; to encourage wide independent reading and investigation (rarely true "research"); and to encourage independent work, such as writing, art, or crafts.

If your children usually have no homework, are getting good marks, and often are busy at home working on their own achievement activities, be grateful and give good feedback. If they have no homework and are doing poorly at school, discuss it with them, and be sure the teachers know that the children could take on more work. If they have too much homework so that it interferes seriously with their health, the balance of their lives, or any independent goal-oriented behavior, discuss it with the child involved and encourage the child to discuss it with the teacher; or, after talking with the child, ask for a parent-student-teacher conference.

If the homework seems to your child to be purposeless, "boring," merely worthless routine, raise the question: "What is the purpose of this work?" That will encourage the child to tie the homework in with achievement goals and to see it in a context of achievement. If the homework really is boring and seemingly worthless, and if the external pressure from school requires it anyway, raise questions at school or encourage your children to do so, respectfully, politely, and purposefully.

Some parents (and teachers) worry about students doing homework together, or conferring about in on the telephone. Certainly if "together" means one student doing the work *for* another it will not develop the achievement motivation of the one who is simply copying the work of the other. But remember that a characteristic of achievers is that they know how to find and use help when they need it, help that strengthens them. Often a five-minute telephone conference (or a quick visit to a neighbor/classmate) on a puzzling math or science problem, or on a difficult question about an English or history assignment, can result in a quick, achievement-motivated advance in understanding for which there might not always be a chance in a large class.

The same can be said for parents helping their children. A

vast amount of excellent, one-on-one instruction or problem-solving is accomplished between parent and child. Just be sure that it doesn't get to the point where the boy whispers out the door to his friend, "I can't play now; I'm helping my father do my homework."*

■ Marks and Achievers

A number of studies have shown that people who are highly motivated to achieve do get marks in school and college higher than those who are not. However, this is not always the case, and knowing why can help improve teaching at school and the support of schoolwork at home.

Earlier I explained that people highly motivated to achieve desire to do a good job, and a better and better job, on tasks that lead to challenging goals, goals they set for themselves or accept for themselves and make their own. High achievers do not see high marks as *the* most important goal in school and college. To accept high marks as a goal, they must be convinced that high marks are related to a worthwhile effort and are a step toward achieving more vital long-range goals, such as promotion, admission to college, or getting a challenging job. Therefore, if schoolwork is seen by achievers mainly as doing meaningless, routine, easy tasks, and if marks are based largely on doing these tasks neatly, regularly, and cooperatively, with no awkward questions asked (7 ÷ 2 = 3½!; what's the point of this assignment?; I already know this. May I read a book instead or work on my experiment?), the achievers may simply be turned off by their own moti-

*There are some books that help students become more independent in achieving basic educational goals, so that they don't have to lean on you or the teacher but can move ahead on their own. Four that I know well, because I wrote them, are:
How to Achieve Competence in English, New York: Bantam Books 1976, 1982.
Improve Your Own Spelling, Wellesley Hills, Mass.: Independent School Press, 1977.
You Are the Editor, Belmont, Cal.: Fearon Pitman Learning, Inc., 1981.
Learning to Achieve (with David McClelland), Glenview, Il.:, Scott, Foresman & Co., 1984.

vation to achieve more important goals. They may settle for passing grades in order to have time for important achievements.

If your children are in such a situation, it requires talking about some questions: How important are good grades to the achievement of your long-range goals? Are there ways you and the teachers can think of that give you more-challenging tasks that will move you toward your goals? Is the situation OK as it is, with you getting by at school with good but not excellent marks, allowing you time for achievements really important to you? Usually, these are not easy questions to answer, but they are always worth discussing.

■ *Putting It into Practice*

1. If you have children in school who have homework, talk over together whether there have been any times when the homework seemed too hard, too easy, or not worth doing. Did this cause any problems? How did the children deal with them? Were they able to make the homework "their own"—to fit it in with their own capacities and goals? If so, how? If not, what happened? Would you and your children agree with this statement? *You should do your homework as it's assigned, to the best of your ability, and no matter what.*

2. Discuss with your children whatever experiences any of you can remember where activities and assignments at school really stimulated the children to achieve and to set further goals.

3. Discuss any experiences that were achievement squelchers. How were they dealt with?

4. With any members of the family who are interested, draw up a set of school rules that you agree would be good ones.

An alternative would be for parents to draw up a set of rules and for school-age children to do the same, without advance discussion. Then compare and discuss the sets of rules and try to agree on which rules should be on a master set. Then get a statement of the rules of the children's present school or schools, and discuss the differences between your rules and the school rules. Would it be desirable to try working to have any rules changed?

Discuss this statement: *You should obey a school rule, even a bad one, until you can get it changed.*

5. Discuss with your children whichever of these questions are appropriate for their age:

(a) What were your feelings when you first entered school? What things surprised you most? Was it better or worse than you thought it would be? Explain.

(b) Talk about the same questions with a child who entered a new school, or a new grade in the same school.

(c) Do you think school has helped make you into more or less of a person who is enthusiastic about getting things done and done well? Try to think of examples of experiences that stimulated your desire to achieve, and things that squelched it. Were the achievement-squelching experiences, if any, necessary because of what schools are required to do? Explain.

6. Here are four situations in which school requirements seem to a student to conflict with, or at least get in the way of, his or her independently set achievement goal. Think about and discuss how the situation could best be dealt with.

(a) Lili, who is in sixth grade, enjoys writing stories. According to her teachers in fourth and fifth grades, and also to her classmates who read them, her stories are unusually good. Therefore, she set a goal for sixth grade to write at least ten stories, have them read, criticized, and corrected, and then to make them into a booklet to share with students in younger grades. Her problem is that the sixth-grade teacher has a requirement that before students do any extra writing, they must pass a test on a list of 150 spelling demons. Lili has studied and studied these demons, but she is not a strong speller and after half the school year has gone she still cannot master the list of words. The teacher has said, "No more stories until you master the 150 spelling demons. That must be your first achievement."

(b) Sharon, in ninth grade, wants very much to learn how to operate a word-processing computer, and she has set this as a goal for this school year. However, priority on the few word processors in school is given to tenth, eleventh, and twelfth graders, and so many of them want to use the processor that there is no time for Sharon, except third period on Mondays, Wednesdays and Fridays, 10:10–10:55, when only a few students are signed up and Sharon could be assigned to a processor. Unfortunately, at that period every day the ninth grade is required to take a special unit on study habits. Sharon's study habits are excellent: she uses her time well, has a good vocabulary, knows how to organize papers, reports, and projects, etc., and no one denies this. But her adviser says, "I'm sorry, but the study habits unit is required of all students and we can't make exceptions."

(c) Jon-Paul's goal is to earn a place on the neighborhood basketball team, which plays in an all-city league. Jon-Paul is an excellent player, but he has to practice with the squad in order to make the team. His problem is this: He's an average student and wants to do well and pass all his courses. The basketball team always practices in the evening, when Jon-Paul should be doing his homework. However, in the afternoons the school conducts a required physical fitness program. If Jon-Paul could be excused from this, he could do his homework in the afternoons and be able to strive for his basketball goal. He rates very high on all the fitness tests. However, the vice principal of the school refuses to excuse him, saying, "If we excuse one student, we'll have to excuse anyone who asks. I'm sorry."

(d) Max, in tenth grade, is very good at mechanical things and has set as a goal to learn enough about auto mechanics, and especially tuning up motors, so that he can get a job in the summer and earn money to put aside for advanced vocational school after he graduates from high school. Half a block from his school is an auto repair garage, and the mechanic there is willing to give Max some work experience every day from 2:15 till 3:00 o'clock— that is, between the end of Max's last class and the time the school bus leaves to take Max home. This work experience, if he does well at it, would put Max in a strong position to get a job. However, the school requires all students to spend the 2:15–3:00 period in school in a special quiet study period doing homework or reading. Max knows he can read and do his homework at home, and he always completes his assignments on time. However, the head teacher of tenth grade says that she is sure he will benefit more from the quiet study period, and that reading is more important than auto mechanics. Therefore, she will not allow him to take the job training.

7. Discuss this question: Why should a student work hard to get good marks? Would you say it is almost always the brightest, hardest-working people who get the best marks? Do you think there is anything more important in school than getting good marks?

8. Arrange to visit your child's school for at least half a day, preferably one whole day (but probably not his or her own classes unless the child and teacher both agree it's O.K.). As you visit, or afterwards, jot down a few things that especially impressed you. Particularly note any activities or classes in which the students seemed especially turned on or to be working especially well to achieve important goals. When there is a relaxed time, tell your child about the visit and compare your impressions with the child's experiences.

9. Jorge, a seventh grader, was out in the school hall when he was required to be in class or study hall. One of his teachers saw him, and at the same moment he ran away from her and into a study room full of students quietly doing homework. The teacher gave chase, entered the study room, and grabbed Jorge. There was a moment of dramatic silence, and then Jorge shouted, "Help! Help! Reality's got me by the arm!"

Do you think Jorge and the teacher behaved in the best way? What did Jorge mean by "reality"? Would the "reality" of obeying the rule have squelched Jorge's achievement motivation? Explain.

10. The poet Robert Frost once said, "The good teacher knows how to get more out of a student by surrounding him with an atmosphere of expectation than by putting the screws on him."

What do you think Frost meant by "expectations" and "the screws"? Do you agree with Frost? Explain.

Afterword

It's Not Inborn; It's Never Too Late; It's Very Important

In the last two chapters, I perhaps overemphasized children's need to learn to work hard on good goals set by others and, in many situations, to accept and make the best of imposed rules and requirements. But I hope you will remember that the habits of conformity and obedience do not make achievers, nor do they strongly motivate people to do a good job, set challenging goals, and strive for them with intelligently calculated independence. The world needs more Origins, not more Pawns.

How do we parents raise children to achieve?

Recall: We enjoy our children; we love them; we encourage them; we spend time with them; we praise their good jobs; we give them freedom to experiment; we are patient with their mistakes while at the same time setting the essential limits that will provide safety and the routines needed for living with others.

When our children are very young, in their first year, say, we do what the University of Denver psychologist Kurt Fisher recommends: "Don't worry about teaching as much as providing a rich and emotionally supportive atmosphere." For the first year or two, we *nurture* our kids: love them, hold them, release them, smile at them, talk to them, play with them, encourage them. Again, I recommend the book *Learningames* for specific, easy suggestions of ways to do all this.

But what if you are a single parent and have to go out to work and then come home and do housework, and cook, and get some time for your own renewal? If that is the situation, try to find a richly supporting daycare center—not a child warehouse based mainly on order and routines. For "underprivileged" children, such centers, we find, raise the confidence of children, raise their IQ scores, help them feel and act like achieving people, because they are given freedom to discover and achieve in stimulating, yet secure surroundings.

■ *Achievement Motivation Not Inborn*

Recently, I met again a former seventh grade pupil of mine who is now in early middle age and has been very successful in just about everything he has undertaken. Somebody remarked about him, "Boy, that Ben is a born achiever!" The incident reminded me just how deeply held the belief is that the urge to achieve is born in people, not developed or trained; that somehow it is just a part of some people's nature. So I decided to write Ben a letter and ask him to tell me how he thinks he became such an achiever or whether it was just born in him. He answered:

> My personal achievements seem to be supported by:
> —confidence in my ability to be "successful";
> —high expectations of myself;
> —impatient curiosity and resourcefulness;
> —willingness to take risks.
> What made me this way? The major factor was early and enduring parental support of my many pursuits: art, animals, automobiles, etc. This developed in me the conviction that I could succeed at anything to which I applied myself. My parents' messages were clear: you are special; you can try new things; you will succeed. Failure will come not from lack of ability but from lack of effort.

Lest Ben seem to you to be merely a hard-working drudge, I quote the next paragraph of his letter:

> I have never been a disciplined person. I aggressively seek the easy way out. But being successful takes precedence over my predisposition to sloth. Since I chose a career which was challenging [Ben works in the sales section of a computer company], and since I was motivated to achieve, I have ended up working as hard as any disciplined person I know, and enjoying it.

Broader evidence that achievement motivation is not inborn but developed is plentiful. In his *The Achieving Society,* David McClelland cites many examples of groups of peoples who, with no known change in their genetic make-up, and with no changes in the composition of the population, changed over the years from low-achieving societies to high-achieving ones, and back again. I cite one example, greatly simplified. Ancient Greek society, motivated to achieve, became so prosperous that the rich entrepreneurs could afford to own slaves to care for all the needs of their children. Each child had a nurse and a pedagogue. Consequently, the children were ''spoiled,'' did not have to strive for what they needed, and therefore did not develop achievement motivation. When they grew up, they were not enterprising, and the prosperity and economic vigor of Greek society declined.

■ *It's Never Too Late*

Again in McClelland and his associates' work, there are examples of older students in school and college receiving achievement training, and rather quickly becoming more productive. This late achievement training worked among all races and classes of people, in rural and urban areas. It also worked among businessmen in many nations all over the world. Training in self-study, goal setting, planning, methods of striving, and measuring progress and evaluating efforts turned many low achievers into high achievers.

Thus, no matter how you may have treated your children (or teachers their students) over the years, it is not too late to shift to achievement training. The earlier the better, yes, but it's never too late.

■ It's Very Important

I have already said that motivation to achieve can be considered "the basic basic." It makes us productive; it urges us to improve things; it develops in us feelings of satisfaction with tasks well done, goals well accomplished; it develops our self-respect, without which we have difficulty respecting others; it does not remove our respect for the past, but it does give us "a sense of the future," and a feeling of responsibility for the future.

The efforts of achievers will make the world better. By raising children to achieve, we can help make the world better, starting right where we are, in our families and in our schools.

■ Putting It into Practice

1. A coat of arms was designed for soldiers or families to wear or display in order to show where they came from and what they stood for. Make up a personal Achievement Coat of Arms to illustrate some important ideas or facts about you, all having to do with achievement. Draw it somewhat in this shape, on a large

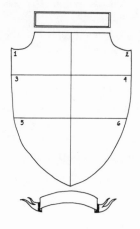

sheet of paper. Fill the numbered spaces with *drawings,* as simple or elaborate as you wish, in color or black and white.

Space 1: two things you are very good at doing
Space 2: your greatest achievement in life to date
Space 3: two things you'd like to be better at
Space 4: the main goal you are striving for right now (long-range or short-range) or expect to be striving for within a year
Space 5: what you hope to be twenty-five years from now, especially what you hope to be achieving
Space 6: eight words that accurately describe the sort of person you are

You may want first to sketch your achievement coat of arms and then draw it more carefully later so that it can be posted on the wall. If each member of the family draws a coat of arms, they can all be posted and you can talk about them.

Either write or be prepared to explain what you drew or wrote in each of the six spaces.

Another thing that is fun, and can lead to some good thinking, is to draw a coat of arms for someone else and explain it.

2. On pages 175–77 are drawings of some people. Look at each picture and then tell (or write) three stories about it.

one story as if the people in it were strong in *affiliation motivation* (a desire to like and be liked by other people and to establish friendships)
one story as if the people in it were strong in *power motivation* (a desire to feel strong, to influence others, to be boss, to run things)
one story as if the people were strong in *achievement motivation* (a desire to set challenging goals and do a good job achieving them)

Tell what you imagine the people are thinking, saying, and doing or expecting to do. Share and talk about your stories with members of your family or others.

Putting It into Practice

To make it clear what you are to do, here are three sample stories based on the first picture:

■ *Affiliation Motivation Story*

Five classmates who don't know each other very well have met on the street after school. The girl with the bag is offering each of the others an apple from the supply she just bought at the store and saying, "I thought you might like an apple. They're good!" The girl sitting on the carton is saying, "I love apples! Gee, you're great!" The boy standing just behind them is thinking, "That's nice of Ellie. Maybe I'll ask them all to come to my house for a while so we can talk and get to know each other better." The guy with his arms out is coming to get an apple and feeling very happy to be a part of such a nice bunch of people, because he usually has a hard time making friends. The girl on the steps, June, is holding a school magazine. Before Ellie offered the apples, June was about to tell one of the people how great she thought his story in the magazine is and suggest that they all read it aloud together. They're all having a good time and hate the idea that they've got a lot of homework to do.

■ *Power Motivation Story*

The names of these people, left to right, are Angie, Roberto, Mary, Dick, and Ruth. All of them want to get elected president of their club. They all want to have real influence and run things, so the club will be the best. Angie is handing out candy bars and saying, "Take one of these if you'll vote for me." Roberto is just waiting till things quiet down so that he can make a little speech telling why he'll be the best president. Mary is saying, "I'll take a candy bar and vote for you, but *only* if you'll make me treasurer." Dick sees a bunch of kids coming down the street and is about to go to where they are and tell them that Angie's nice but that *he* really knows how to run things. He'll explain how he was captain of the school wrestling team and also knows the principal of the school very well, so he'll have influence. As for Ruth, she's not paying attention. Instead, she's counting the number of signatures she has of people who have promised to vote for her, and then she'll use that to show others that they, too, should vote for her.

■ *Achievement Motivation Story*

All these people are waiting at a bus stop. The girl on the steps is studying her science book for a few minutes before going into the store to buy what she needs to bake a cake that night. The boy with his arms out is reciting lines for a play in order to improve his performance. The girl with the bag is showing how many aluminum cans she was able to collect in a drive to keep the street clean and earn money for a science project. The girl sitting is saying, "That's great!" and thinking about what plans they could make to collect even more cans or money. The boy standing is not really listening to what's going on. He's thinking hard about how to improve his lay-up shots in basketball and has just had an idea for a special way of turning his body.

3. In this book, I've tried to show that it's very important that children be raised to be achievers, that being motivated to achieve is "the basic basic." It would be interesting to let each member of the family who is old enough to be able to do so write a brief argument, say about 150–200 words long, supporting this statement: *It is important to raise and educate people so that they will be highly motivated to achieve.* For children who are not old enough to write a paper, an alternative activity would be to think up all the possible points that support the statement, maybe jotting down a key word or making a little drawing to remind the young person of each idea. It would be good for parents to write their own papers, too. Then, when there is time, share the papers and spoken arguments, and discuss them. You may find that people are saying, "Yes, but. . . ." That leads to the next practice.

4. Write down (or be ready to tell) the arguments *against* raising and educating people to achieve. Share and discuss these.

5. Discuss this question, or write about it, or draw pictures about: Is our family raising people to achieve? Let each person think of as many specific examples as possible of the way people behave—what they do and how they relate to each other—that

help to answer the question. The discussion might even lead to the question: "Are there any things that should be changed in the way we live in this family? If there are, how can they be changed?" And a last question might be, "What are we doing *right?*" Think of examples. Perhaps a set of posters or large-printed statements could be made of these things and put up somewhere for a time, just to keep the discussion going.

About the Author

ERIC W. JOHNSON, a graduate of Germantown Friends School, Harvard College, and the Harvard Graduate School of Education (Master of Arts in Teaching), has taught English, history, and sex education in a number of independent and public schools, grades 5-12, for more than 25 years. He was headmaster of Friends' Central School, in Overbrook, Pa., and has worked as head of the junior high school and director of development at Germantown Friends School, in Philadelphia, where he is now Clerk of the School Committee (chairman of the board, in non-Quaker parlance). At present, he writes, advises schools, and consults with teachers, administrators, and parents on various educational matters. Some of the books he has written are *Life into Language, How To Achieve Competence in English, How To Live through Junior High School, Love and Sex in Plain Language,* and *An Introduction to Jesus of Nazareth.* He is coauthor of *Language for Daily Use, Love and Sex and Growing Up,* and *The Family Book about Sex.*

INDEX